THE TWIN ENIGMA

THE TWIN ENIGMA
An Exploration of Our Enduring Fascination with Twins

Vivienne Lewin

KARNAC

First published in 2016 by
Karnac Books Ltd
118 Finchley Road
London NW3 5HT

British Library Cataloguing in Publication Data

A C.I.P. for this book is available from the British Library

ISBN-13: 978-1-78220-477-0

Typeset by Medlar Publishing Solutions Pvt Ltd, India

www.karnacbooks.com

For Saul, without whose sustained interest in my ideas and repeated prompting to write, this book would not have emerged.

And to Jacob and Sofia who offer living confirmation of the nature of twin relationships.

CONTENTS

ACKNOWLEDGEMENTS

Many people have communicated with me since publishing my earlier book, *The Twin in the Transference* (2004), thanking me and confirming my understanding of twin relationships, and offering new ideas about twins. I want to thank them for stimulating me and prompting me to extend the areas of research that I have incorporated in this new book about twins.

I want to express special appreciation to the late Elizabeth Bryan who, in addition to encouraging and advising me, gave me access to her own archives on twins.

Elizabeth Pector has generously allowed me to quote her poem, Footprints, written after the death of one of her twin children.

I had some correspondence with the late Charlotte Williams while she was writing her book, *Black Valley* (2014), and she sent me her personal material about separating from her twin sister. Her husband, John Williams, has generously given me permission to use this in this book.

Rick Morgan Jones has been a stalwart supporter of my work on twins, helping me explore and deepen my understanding of the early preverbal sensate memories that are so important in the twin relationship.

Finally, I want to thank Oliver Rathbone and his team at Karnac Books for agreeing to publish this book, and for his continuing support of my work.

INTRODUCTION

Twins excite all sorts of feelings and responses in most people, and are a source of considerable interest both scientifically and in everyday life. When I first started writing about twins, it seemed that anyone I told had a story to tell me about twins—something fantastical, magical, quirky, or just odd. Any mother of twins will recount how she is often stopped in the street and asked if the babies are twins, usually followed with, "Are they identical?" regardless of whether the babies look alike and are of the same sex. I believe there are deep-seated reasons for this fascination with twins and our desire to find "identical soulmates".

So why write this book about twins?

This book is different because I offer an understanding of the deep unconscious factors that are active in twin development and in our perception of twins. It is not a "how to" book about bringing up twins, but rather a guide to our understanding of the twin relationship and our fascination with twins that may help parents, clinicians, and the twins themselves to facilitate maximal development for the twins as individuals within a valued twin relationship.

In 2004 I wrote *The Twin in the Transference* (republished 2014, Karnac) in which I explored the deeper, unconscious aspects of being a twin, of having twin children, and of our attitudes towards twins. My aim was to try to understand more about the particular dynamics that affect twins in their individual development, in their relationship, and what it is that so excites us about twins.

I have had numerous requests since writing my first book to write something simpler, more accessible, about my understanding of the twin relationship. I have also been approached by twins, and by parents of twins, who have told me that they were relieved to read my book because they found it offered a deep understanding of the twin relationship and its implications for development, and for the relationships between twins with other significant people in their lives.

Many books have been written about twins, a large number of these written by a twin, either to celebrate twinship, or to commemorate or compensate for the loss of a twin, whether before birth, or postnatally, at any and all ages. Parents of twins write about their experience of bringing up twins, both the pleasures and difficulties that they encounter.

Psychotherapists and psychologists have written about developmental issues with twins, and how parents should treat them, among them being Joan Friedman, Barbara Klein, Joan Woodward, and Audrey Sandbank—many of whom are themselves a twin. In fact, scientists of *all* descriptions have studied twins for decades in the hope of learning the secrets of inheritability and the progress of both individual development and diseases.

And of course children's books explore the many facets and functions of a phantasy twin through the twinships and imaginary friends of the children in the story. Twins feature with a particular prominence in literature and films and I will examine some of these to see what it is about the twin relationship that draws so much attention.

With the wealth of available "how to" books relating to twins, I will be focusing my attention elsewhere—at our fascination with twins, the source of this, the underlying unconscious dynamics at work, how these dynamics will affect the development of the twins, and what effect our relationships with twins will have on their development as individuals within a twin relationship.

So, what is the source of this fascination with twins? This is an important question and I will attempt to offer an understanding of the deep unconscious factors that influence us in thinking in particular ways about twins and illustrate it with examples from real life and literature.

Why is this understanding so important? The number of twins is on the increase and we need to be much clearer about twins, twinning and twin relationships and our attitudes to them, for their and our healthy development. Both in vitro fertilisation (IVF) treatment and the increasing numbers of mothers having babies at a later age have influenced the number of twins being born. Factors that affect the rate of twin births may include genetics, the places where people live, and age-related factors. The rates of dizygotic (DZ—commonly called "fraternal") twin births is increasing as a result of more than one baby being implanted during IVF treatment. Monozygotic (MZ—commonly but erroneously called "identical") twinning may be generated by genetic factors, but it can also result from an increased tendency to splitting of the embryo after fertility treatment.[1]

With this increase in the numbers of twins and the special significance that they have for us, we need to know more about how we see twins, and why we see them this way. We need to use this information to understand how being a twin influences the development of each of the twin babies and their relationships with others in their world.

Twins have a particular bond, and they are frequently encouraged to develop as a twin pair rather than individually. Having twins is sometimes regarded as a relief for mother, as they may provide companionship for each other, and they may play with and entertain each other, thus taking some strain off her, especially as she has so much extra work to do. To some extent, this may be helpful to the twins. But it can be damaging when there is not sufficient emotional space and encouragement given to each child in its relationship especially with the mother, and the father and siblings, to enable each twin to develop a unique and individual personality.

There are specific positive aspects about being a twin as well as the difficulties that having twin children engenders. There are also particular qualities that we project onto twins because of what twins represent to each of us at a deep unconscious level, psychically. Twins may experience an unparalleled closeness and understanding, though this is not necessarily so. They may also be intimately connected in rivalry and hatred in an equally binding way.

The twin relationship is particular and I will explore it in this book. The extraordinary intimacy and closeness between twins represent the special factors in twin relationships that are highly prized by the twins, and also by the parents of twins. Singletons envy this "special factor" as they perceive that twins have something exciting that they do not have, and that we all long for. This is so even though being a twin may create developmental difficulties for these "special siblings". These perceived special qualities have deep roots in us all and I will offer my understanding of their origins in Chapter One.

It is very important for both parents of twins, and clinicians whether they are engaged in IVF treatment or developmental work with twins, to have a thorough understanding of the twin relationship. We need to know more about the possibilities and difficulties in twin development, and of the significance of the twin relationship for healthy growth in each of the children. Parents and clinicians need a great understanding of the twin dynamics and our approach to twins so that they can enable twins to develop individually as well as within the twin relationship.

There is a basic premise underlying all my work on twins: I believe that no two people are identical, not even monozygotic (so-called "identical") twins. To believe that they are identical feeds our phantasies about finding twin souls and is designed to avoid recognition of twins' differences and separateness, whatever the genetic make-up of the twins. In all twin pairs, there are, to a greater or lesser extent, genetic, psychological and behavioural differences, as well as the much-heralded similarities. Each twin will have to struggle with her own individual processes of development to carve out a personal sense of identity, as well as recognising the importance of the twin relationship. For each twin, their individuality will overlap to varying degrees with that of the other twin, and this may lead to aspects of a shared identity. This overlapping, shared area of identity between twins will form the core of their indelible sense of connection throughout their lives. It will have started before birth and continue throughout their development.

Recent research has thrown new light on the factors that affect twin development and relationships. This is especially so with new research in genetics[2] and epigenetics.[3] Monozygotic (MZ) twins develop from a single fertilised egg fertilised by one sperm, and they may or may not share a placenta and amniotic sac. Seventy to seventy-five per cent share one placenta and have individual amniotic sacs, while twenty-five to thirty per cent have completely separate sacs and placentas. One to two per cent of MZ twins share both placenta and amniotic sac and are at greater risk than are other twin foetuses. Humans have twenty-three chromosome matched pairs. MZ twins are almost always of the same sex, though there have been rare ooccasions where one MZ twin is male (having forty-six chromosomes including an XY chromosome) while the other twin is female (having forty-five chromosomes plus one X chromosome—i.e. lacking the forty-sixth Y chromosome). Dizygotic twins (DZ) develop from two separate fertilised eggs fertilised by two sperms, and usually have separate placentas and amniotic membranes. However, the placentas of DZ twins might be fused, resulting in twins that are monochorionic (one placenta) and diamniotic (two amniotic sacs).

All monozygotic twins are genetically different in some aspects, despite having come from the same fertilised egg and the fact that most are very similar in appearance (Hall, 2003). Various intra-uterine factors account for this differential development: the timing of the twinning process; initial differences in the number of cells at the time of separation of the egg into two; differences in blood flow to each twin; different types of placental attachment; the amount of space for each twin in utero; hormones and chemical factors that influence the development of each embryo. Twin transfusion syndrome in MZ twins sharing a placenta can cause very uneven environments for the twins and may be fatal for one or both babies. Unequal prenatal nutrition in MZ or DZ twins may depend in part on the attachment and placement of the placentas. As mentioned above, there may be chromosomal changes caused by epigenetic factors, and the distribution patterns of X chromosomes in twin girls may differ. I will explore this in greater detail in Chapter Two.

Lawrence Wright, in his excellent book *Twins. Genes, Environment and the Mystery of Identity* (1997) raises the question as to whether MZ and DZ twinning have something in common, as both types of twins are more alike than singleton siblings. Twinning is no longer simply regarded as of two types—MZ and DZ. Rather, the resemblance between MZ and DZ twins exists along a continuum. So not only are MZ twins not identical, but there is also a third type of twin—fraternal twins that develop from a single egg that splits before conception, and each split embryo is then fertilised by two different sperms. Sometimes the only certain way to determine the zygosity of twins is by genetic testing.

The so-called "vanishing twin syndrome", where twins are conceived but one disappears before birth, is common in twin pregnancies, especially in the early stages. There have also been incidents where one DZ twin becomes absorbed into the other in utero, creating a human chimera. Reports of the discovery of an undeveloped twin inside the body of a live twin generally create great excitement in the press. Occasionally, a tiny, fully formed dried-out lifeless foetus may be attached to the placenta of a live baby—it is the remains of the dead twin and is known as "foetus papyraceus".

Opposite sex twins are often regarded as psychodynamically different from other twins, perhaps not as real twins. Their relationship is expected to be less enmeshed and more like ordinary brother and sister, assuming that the gender difference creates an immediate separateness between them from the start. It is my view that the twin relationship between opposite sex twins would not be substantially different from that of same sex DZ twins, since many of the developmental factors that they encounter are similar. Most importantly, the early pre-verbal relationship between the twins, in utero and soon after birth is just as powerful and indelible for opposite-sex twins as it is for any other twins, though there may be additional binding factors for MZ twins in utero, as I discuss in Chapter Two.

The processes of individual development and separateness for opposite sex twins will depend on many factors, as it does for other twins, on their psychic development, constitutional factors, parental and other attitudes to the twin babies, and a deep understanding that each baby is an individual in its own right, as well as being a twin.

A documentary film called *Lone Twin*, made by Anna van de Wee in 2012, about opposite sex twins, highlights the similarities with other twins. To varying degrees the twin pairs exhibited an enmeshed twin relationship in which the other opposite sex twin was felt to be a twin soul, an indispensible part of the self. Absence of one twin caused considerable anxiety to the remaining twin. As with same sex twins, the loss of an opposite sex twin results in severe experiences of loss of part of the self, and lone twin finds it difficult to mourn, successfully, the lost twin. I believe that this is so because of the narcissistic nature of the enmeshed twin relationship as I will explore in Chapter Two.

The special and different ways in which twins are perceived in mythology and in cultural practices throughout the world, have been much observed. Twins may be regarded as god-like or, alternatively, evil. There is a wide divergence of customs regarding twins and their birth, and in the way both the twins and their mother, and in some cases the whole family, is perceived. I will examine some aspects of this in Chapter Five.

In Chapter One, The twin in ourselves—intra-twin dynamics, I explore the source of our fascination with twins, the experience of longing for a twin that we all encounter—the twin in ourselves (the phantasy twin). This examination of the intra-twin dynamic will focus on the deeper unconscious issues that affect both the development of twin identity and our fascination with twins.

Chapter Two, Twins together—inter-twin dynamics, examines the developmental issues encountered by twins and their families, and the evolution of the inter-twin dynamics. Again the focus will be on the deeper issues that affect the relationships of twins and our relationships with them, including the phantasy twin, the dynamics between the twins, and those between each of the twins and their parents, their siblings, and the wider world.

In Chapter Three, Twins apart, I will explore the issues particular to twins that influence the development of separateness for each of them, and the importance of the indelible twin relationship. It will also examine the devastating sense of loss a surviving twin experiences when the other twin dies. This understanding will again be rooted in the deeper issues in twin development.

Chapter Four, Twins in society, will look at our perceptions of twins through their fame or notoriety, the way the twins and the media use the twin relationship to generate excitement, and how this expresses our enduring fascination with twins.

Chapter Five, Twins around the world—twin mythology, beliefs, and cultural practices, will focus on twins in the wider world, and how they are regarded and treated based on local religious and cultural beliefs. I will explore how legends, myths, and bible stories express and create a narrative for our unconscious world, with particular reference to twins and twinning.

In Chapter Six, Twins and doubles in literature, I will focus on twins from Shakespeare's twins in his life and his plays, to the use of twin relationships and doubles in later and in contemporary literature. I will look at the understanding we can gain of the dynamics of twinning and how we perceive twins, from the ways in which twins are used in literature.

Finally, in the concluding comments, I will outline the main themes that emerge from this wide-ranging exploration of twin relationships and how we perceive twins, how this knowledge highlights the need for a greater understanding of twins and their relationships, and the way our fascination with twins can blind us to the realities about twins. The developmental tasks for twins differ in particular respects from those of singletons, and a better understanding will aid the twins themselves and all connected with them in their growth towards maturity.

Notes

1. For the sake of brevity and convenience, I will throughout this book refer to twins as MZ (monozygotic—single-egg twins) and DZ (dizygotic—two-egg twins). I do not use the terms "identical" and "fraternal" for twins because, as I explore in Chapter Two, no two twins are ever "identical". Where I do use the term "identical" in relation to twins, it is either a quote or it refers to dynamic processes and not the genetic status of the twins.
2. Genetics is the study of heredity and the variation of inherited characteristics, based on our understanding of the sequence of different genes and their impact on development.
3. Epigenetics is the study of changes in the way genes are expressed, as a result of factors (chemical, hormonal, or environmental) rather than changes in the underlying DNA.

CHAPTER ONE

The twin in ourselves: intra-twin dynamics

The main focus of this book is on twins and twinning processes—our perception of twins, their development, both psychically and developmentally, and as a twin pair—and the internal dynamics that play an active part in the binding qualities of the twin relationship. Twins have to negotiate the same processes of emotional development as do singletons, but they have also to deal with the fact of being a twin, and all the factors that will affect their individual development and their twinship.

The heart of the matter

There are deep unconscious issues that affect both the twin relationship and our perception of it. Twins both fascinate and disturb us, and we tend to attribute special qualities to their relationship. In this chapter I want to look at how we idealise the twin relationship, how we project properties onto them that are our own, and are based on our own early experiences in life, and how this affects development in twins.

All multiples are felt to be odd and exciting in some way, but twins seem to generate a specific kind of interest. There are annual twin events both large and small where what seems to excite attention about the twins attending is not their individuality, differences, or the duality within a pair of twins, but their unity as a pair. They dress alike, stick together, and are interviewed together by researchers and the press. The frisson as they talk for each other, or finish each other's sentences, is nothing compared with the excitement about the so-called secret languages of twins, or the silent unconscious communication between them that is so highly attuned and is frequently likened to telepathy.

Twins are viewed with awe in many societies, where they may be treated as gifts from the gods, or alternatively as evil omens to be banished or killed, often along with the mother who bore them (see Chapter Five). There is no doubt that twins arouse very primitive feelings in us and we tend to see them in the light of these feelings.

This fascination with twins and the raw excited feelings they arouse, lies in our own earliest experiences. Melanie Klein suggested in 1963 that there is a universal longing to be a twin, which originates in our first experience with our mothers. It is based on the deep unconscious understanding between a mother and her newborn child. Even when circumstances are not optimal, the mother is usually attuned to her baby in a way that enables her to understand the baby's needs and wants without words. She is able to take in from the baby the raw experiences that upset or even terrify the baby, and process them in a way that makes it possible for the baby to re-absorb the altered experience in a way with which it can more easily deal, helping the baby feel understood and contained. This helps the baby begin to develop its own capacities for dealing with life, and so makes the ordinary exigencies of life more manageable to the infant.

The basics of early infant development

I will spend a little time describing the ordinary processes of mental and emotional development that we all go through, to lay the groundwork for a greater understanding of what happens to twins in their development.

In 1956, Donald Winnicott referred to the mother's involvement with her baby as a "primary maternal preoccupation". Whether mother is conscious of it or not, the baby is ever-present in her mind and this enables her to be responsive to her baby in a way that no one else can. It is the mother who is able to bear the terrifying anxieties her infant experiences and who is able to make the world a safer place for the baby. She is able to enjoy the baby's intense love as well as tolerate the hate that is generated when life does not run as smoothly as the baby would like.

The baby finds interruptions, gaps, and absences difficult to tolerate with the result that he experiences frustration. If the baby finds this too much to manage, he then directs his rage at his closest objects (usually mother) in a ruthless way. Winnicott suggests that it is only the mother who can tolerate the baby's ruthlessness, responding with love and understanding, and without feeling the need to retaliate. Of course she may be upset or hurt by it, but because of her primal bond with her infant, she can bear it. Where the mother is unable to bear the baby's anxieties and ruthlessness, this may lead to a split in the baby's personality. Then the vengeful ruthless self remains undiluted and unneutralised, and may give rise to sudden eruptions of violent rage or behaviour. We see this darker side of the personality in some people, and exemplified in stories like Dr Jekyll and Mr Hyde.

If the baby has had sufficient "good enough mothering", he will gradually develop a capacity to be alone—he will be able to tolerate gaps in provision without being overwhelmed by frustration or sometimes panic, knowing that mother will be back. The baby develops a sense of being alone but most importantly, alone in relation to another person. This depends on the development of the baby's ability to tolerate both a sense of otherness or separateness from mother, and the ability to be separate from her without feeling overwhelmed by feelings of loss. So the non-perfect, good-enough mother is essential to the baby's development. However, embedded in this welcome development towards individuality there is also a sense of essential loneliness, a sense of loss of a closeness that was there and that can never be replaced.

Neurological studies of the development of the brain in infants (Schore, 1994) have indicated the importance of the early relationship between the baby and the mother. The "gaze" between mother and infant is so familiar to us from seeing mothers with new babies looking into each other's eyes, and can be seen in many artistic portrayals of mother and babies. The "gaze" between infant and mother is an essential means of communication between them. In this shared experience the baby finds a kind of mirroring of himself in mother's eyes that enables him to develop a sense of self. The mutual relationship between this nursing pair is reflected in the way different areas of the brain of the infant develop. Those areas that have been observed to house the emotions and experiences of relatedness to another person, and the memories of those experiences, will develop in response to the actual experience of the infant with its mother. During this time, neuronal networks develop within the brain that lay down the templates for the later development of relationships throughout life. These templates are dynamic, not static, and they do retain a degree of plasticity throughout life, though they are never again quite as open to developmental influences as in the early days of the infant.

Thus we see that the intense visual connectedness between mother and baby is a vital developmental factor, but it is not the only one, as touch, smell, and hearing (the more primitive senses) also play a vital part in the creating of the bond between mother and baby. The closeness of the mother–infant relationship will depend on all these factors for development, and it is within this relationship that healthy development takes place.

Observations of infants with their mothers show that the searching for each other starts very soon after birth. There is a synchronised, very early engagement between the mother–infant couple. Karen Proner wrote in 2000 about a 7-hour-old infant searching for his mother's face and he was able to distinguish her from an observer. The mother's response and her receptivity to her infant will shape the infant's next move—towards or away from her. And this process is not one-way. The mother also seeks out her infant, wanting to find out who he is, thus creating a synchronised "dance" between mother and infant.

The importance of making eye contact has been noted by Farroni, Csibra, Simion, and Johnson in 2002 and by Farroni, Johnson, and Csibra in 2004, among many others. Looking is the most powerful way of establishing a link for communicating between people. From early on, infants learn that the way other people behave has significance for them. Babies from birth onwards are able to distinguish between someone looking either directly at them and looking elsewhere and they prefer a direct gaze. With a mutual direct gaze, the neural activity in the brains of babies is enhanced. This is later reflected in social skills.

This primitive mutual, attuned response between mother and infant is the first form of postnatal communication between them. It is this early contact that creates the sense of oneness so that the mother and baby become attuned to each other. The instinctual interplay between mother and baby stimulates mother's "reverie", the emotional space she creates for the baby, and is a preface to mother's "falling in love" with her infant, and for the infant to feel it belongs.

Alan Schore's (1994) research on brain activity in these early days of the infant–mother relationship indicates that the mother regulates her infant's state of arousal through the bond of unconscious communication between them that leads to rapid matching responses in the mother–infant pair. This interactive matrix facilitates the developing understanding between the mother and infant, and the expression of feelings between them. In this way mother modulates the level of feelings and arousal experienced by the infant. Insufficient modulation of the infant's state of arousal will interfere with its capacity to process information. The infant will seek an optimal level of arousal where it is neither over-excited nor under-stimulated, but can attend to what is going on.

The key to mother's capacity to repair the infant's overly aroused state is her ability to monitor and regulate her own emotional state, particularly her negative feelings, and this leads to "good enough" mothering. Negative emotions in the infant will be minimised and the opportunities for the development of positive feelings will be maximised, as is found in states of play. This would lead the infant to a sense of safety and a positively charged curiosity about life.

The infant's sense of self and its relationship with others build on the base of the patterns that form as a result of inter-relatedness between mother and baby. In this dynamic interactive process, mother and baby influence each other from moment to moment. The structure of these experiences arising from these interactions will help the infant organise its experiences. This is a dynamic framework in which continuous transformations and restructurings take place. The infant's psychic development is in a constant state of active reorganisation as the baby gathers a sense of himself internally.

The patterns of mutual influence between mother and baby will include both the baby's own regulation of its states of arousal (self-regulation), and the interactive regulation provided within the mother–baby dynamic. It will encompass the dimensions of time, space, emotional state and state of arousal. Within the first two months of life, the baby will build primitive internal images of himself based on these interactive patterns that will later form the basis of symbolic representations. Melanie Klein proposed that the infant has an innate curiosity about the world he is in, and it is clear that the baby builds his internal world based not only on his experiences of hunger, pain, and fatigue, but also on his curiosity and wish to explore through play.

Infants are also very attuned to sounds, particularly human voices. They recognise patterns of speech that indicate that they are being addressed specifically. Babies are primed to respond to people. In the first 15 hours after birth they are able to distinguish their mother's voice from others, and they prefer it to a stranger's voice. They also prefer their mother's smell to a stranger's smell and will select their mother's face rather than a stranger's. (Beebe, Lachmann, & Jaffe, 1997) But babies have also learned from their experiences before birth, in utero, as they can recognise repeated and familiar patterns of sounds, smells and taste from that time.

Within the first year of its life, the baby has already developed the capacity to recognise and remember faces, sounds, smells, movements, appropriate behaviour patterns, and what they mean.

It takes some time for the infant to develop his own capacities for putting together the information he receives in a way that has coherence and personal meaning, a narrative informed by current and past events and memories and experiences, i.e. for thinking. The capacity for thinking helps us deal with the world, both inner and outer, assessing the inflow of information, placing it in context, making sense of it, without feeling overwhelmed or experiencing a massive disruption to our sense of self.

Initially the baby is highly dependent on the mother, and father and wider family group, to support him in all his development, including this mental processing about the world. In the very early days, with mother attending to her baby so closely, the baby has yet to develop an understanding of what belongs to himself and what belongs outside— mother, breast, bottle, and so on. It is like developing what Esther Bick, in 1968, called an "emotional skin", an imaginary membrane inside which the infant feels himself to exist, and recognises himself, as separate from elements in the outside world. This emotional skin is permeable, with the result that stimuli from both inside and outside can be communicated. When the infant has had a sufficiently good experience, he will have a clearer sense of what is inside and what is outside, though there are times, especially times of great stress, when there may be something of a mix-up. When this happens, this can lead to a sense of confusion of identity and consequent distress.

The internal twin

The developmental factors described above apply to all infants, whether singletons, twins or other multiples, and they have particular relevance for the development of identity in every baby. For twins the developmental issues are additionally complicated by the actual fact of the presence of another baby of the same age, ever-present in the life and mind of each baby, of mother, father, and other siblings. The presence of another baby will invariably affect the relationships between each infant and mother in the fundamental early stages of development, and later with father and other family members. I will explore this aspect of twin development more fully in the next chapter.

In the early days of an infant's life when he has not yet developed a clear sense of his own identity, there will be a blurring of what the baby imagines is himself and what is mother. As the baby experiences mother's care he creates mental images representing that experience, images that are dynamic and interchangeable according to the variability of the care it receives. These images or unconscious phantasies develop within the interactions between baby and mother, and it is only much later in the infant's development that he can begin to distinguish what is his own. He will learn to recognise his own bodily and mental stimuli, what comes from outside himself, and what that outside source might be. So there is a confusion, not so much of identities but of the source of the satisfaction, frustration, pain, or pleasure that the infant experiences.

So the mother who feeds, cleans, and loves her baby, will initially be felt by the baby, in his imagination, to be part of himself, in a way a twin of himself. I say "twin", because before the infant develops a capacity to distinguish clearly between himself and others, he will see others in his own image, as a twin. As Winnicott wrote in 1971, the precursor of the mirror is the mother's face. What does the infant see when he looks at his mother? He sees himself. The baby creates a "phantasy twin" of himself in an unconscious process.

The experience of so profound an unconscious understanding between mother and baby, the apparently perfect unconscious understanding that is provided by the attuned mother, creates a bond of togetherness between her and baby. It not only lays down the blueprint for all future communications and relationships in the infant's life, it also leaves the each individual baby with a longing to regain this perfect understanding—a longing for the twin that so perfectly understood at a time of his greatest vulnerability and dependency.

The bible story of Adam and Eve being expelled from the Garden of Eden represents this universal longing for a perfect untroubled state of at-oneness. The feeling of an initial innocence and at-oneness with mother/the world is lost at each interruption or break, or in terms of the Garden of Eden, at our awakening knowledge that the state of bliss is temporary, and bound to be curtailed at some point by all sorts of factors like time, tiredness, pain, and so on. We expect to encounter this secure love again, but know it will never again be untainted because we know it is fleeting, it will again end.

It is this longing that forms a deep inner core and pervades our lives, leaving us either seeking the kind of relationship that we hope will again provide this perfect understanding, or alternatively, cutting off in frustration as we lose hope of ever finding it (as may happen in autism).

It is this longing that echoes in our fascination with twins. The ubiquitous longing for a twin is, I believe, at the heart of our fascination with twins. When we encounter twins, we resurrect our own early experiences of at-oneness and project this onto the twin pair. The twins seem to have achieved what we long for, and the sight of them stimulates our excitement and perhaps our envy. We attribute to them as a couple our experiences and longings emanating from our infantile years, as we spontaneously identify with them. As a result of these projections the twins seem to acquire a rather magical quality. The phantasy of having a twin forms the core of the idealisation of the twin relationship and in this ideal phantasy the twinship is perfect, devoid of feelings of rivalry and jealousy. We believe that twinship provides a relationship of continued deep understanding and sympathy. In reality we know how very far this is from the truth—the twinship creates not only unparalleled companionship, but also vehement rivalry between the twin pair.

Phantasy twins

It is quite common to hear someone wondering if they have lost a twin before birth, convinced that this would explain a persistent feeling of sadness, an unsatisfied longing, a sense of incompleteness that they experience. This may have been true for some, but for many it is more likely to be based on a longing for a phantasy twin as a representative of the early experience of understanding with mother.

I use the word "phantasy", rather than "fantasy", to distinguish between this very primitive unconscious creation by the baby, and a knowing conscious "fantasy" of the more developed mind like the imaginary twins or friends of childhood. A phantasy twin provides the illusion of regaining the perfect untroubled internal state, filling in the gaps, or providing comfort while waiting. The phantasy twin is created by the infant in its own image and is therefore a narcissistic structure.

Twin infants relate not only to mother, but also to each other in a primary relationship. In mother's absence, the sense of loneliness in each twin may be lessened by the presence of the other twin. It is as if the phantasy twin offering perfect understanding and obliterating loneliness, created on the base of the early experience with mother, becomes a reality embodied by the other twin. The other twin comes to represent the phantasy twin. When this happens, the waiting for and anticipation of mother's return is attenuated. The gap is filled with a temporary solution—one that does not actually meet the needs of the infant, but will distract it from having to tolerate and mourn the loss of the perfect mother of phantasy as the other twin occupies the waiting space, acting like a comforter.

Parents readily recognise this, and will often put the twin babies together to comfort each other. As the twins recognise each other's rhythms, and resonate psycho-biologically from the time they were so close in utero, it may indeed be a comfort to find the other twin alongside. But of course the other twin will not satisfy the primary needs of the baby, and he may also be the recipient of the rage and hatred of the mother who is not immediately there to tend to her baby. So the other twin may be at any time a comforter, a rival for mother's attention, or a receptacle for the bad feelings aroused in an always-imperfect situation.

The primary bonding with the other twin is an essential element in the twin relationship. It develops through many factors: the creation and projection into each other of a phantasy twin, the psycho-biological resonances between them, the twinning processes linked with identifying with each other, and external sources such as confusion between the babies by parents and others, the perceptions of others of the twin pair, and so on.

This intimate unconscious twin bond creates the difficulty twins experience in separating from each other even in adult life. The twinning, while comforting, is not a developmental bond. The other twin, unlike the mother, lacks the aspect of a generational gap that is necessary to help the infant grow towards a unique and individual identity. This gap, as experienced with mother, is needed to add differentiation and separateness between the twins, rather than sameness.

The phantasy of having a twin that emanates from both the individual twins themselves, and in the perceptions of others, will play a prominent role in reinforcing the actual twinship. Both external and internal factors interact to create an enduring twin relationship.

Thus our fascination with twins and spontaneous identification with the twin pair is based on our own very early experiences. However, the actual life of twins is not as idyllic or problem-free as we imagine. With the fusion of phantasy and actual twins the twins may become almost inseparable, they may both act as a substitute for an absent parent, and they may provide perfect understanding at both conscious and unconscious levels. But a phantasy twin is not an actual twin. The main difference between them is that in an actual twinship, negative and aggressive feelings, rivalry, and jealousy, are generated and expressed, unlike the untroubled and unchanging relationship with the phantasy twin.

At the heart of our fascination with twins is the fact that the phantasy twin of infancy remains buried at an unconscious level, and is re-awakened by the sight of twins. The very early experiences of the infant establish a blueprint for closeness and intimacy that underlies the longing for a twin self, as well as for later more mature relationships. Our idealisation of twin relationships is based on our own longing for a twin and the perceived attainment of this perfect state by the twin pair we encounter.

Imaginary twins/friends in childhood

As a rather charming example of the universal urge towards twinning, I was told recently of a five-year-old boy with his father. The father was explaining to his son how a sundial works, and the importance of the shadow in telling the time. The boy said he had a shadow, and that his shadow was his twin. It went everywhere with him. He added that his shadow was not only his twin; it was also his imaginary friend. But it was not his only imaginary friend, he explained—he had other imaginary friends like Teddy and some of his other toys.

It is common in childhood that a child will create an imaginary twin or friend. This imaginary twin/friend is not the same as an unconscious phantasy twin of infancy, but it is a manifestation or representation of the phantasy twin of infancy.

There may be many reasons for the creation of an imaginary twin/friend. It is a conscious construction that employs the experience of the phantasy twin of infancy—the child knows the twin/friend is imaginary, even though she may deny it at the time. She will talk about the imaginary twin, talk to it, play with it, and may use it in a variety of ways. It represents aspects of the child's longings, or feelings that are split off and placed outside. Both the phantasy twin of infancy and the imaginary friend of childhood are based on processes of splitting of the self and projection of the split off part of the self into an imaginary other, but it is important to distinguish between them. A phantasy twin is an unconscious creation of the infant and remains embedded at deep layers within us all, generating a longing for perfect union with another. An imaginary friend is a conscious creation mostly used as a temporary solution by children to manage difficult situations, and later relinquished.

Imaginary friends may be used to alleviate loneliness either when the child is alone, or as a representation of the essential loneliness we all experience as described above. A child may create an imaginary friend when trying to cope with the loss of a love-object that is temporarily unavailable or lost forever. With such a loss, the child experiences a loss of aspects of herself and hopes to regain these lost aspects of the self by creating the imaginary twin. The imaginary friend may fill the gap and enable the child to manage difficult feelings, of anxiety or discomfort until these can be dealt with at a later time. Thus the creation of an imaginary friend may be used as a transitional stage in development, until the child feels able to tolerate the feelings of loss and relinquish control of the object.

The imaginary friend may also be used more defensively, to avoid knowing about loneliness or loss. This may be a helpful temporary solution in that it allows the child to retain a sense of herself through a difficult time, until her place in the world can be regained. However, where the imaginary friend is used as a longer-term refuge from the reality of loss, and where this persists into adulthood, this may be damaging to mature development.

Another common use of imaginary friends is to resolve ambivalent feelings that the child struggles to accommodate alongside each other within himself. He does this by assigning some of his conflicting feelings to the imaginary friend—for example, Peter says he does not like his new sister. The child thus disowns his own feelings of dislike for his new sister and so manages his guilt and fear of punishment. The imaginary friend might thus represent the other side of an emotional conflict and can be used to express "unacceptable feelings" like anger and hatred. The child will then feel able to maintain the unity within himself.

The imaginary friend is felt to be someone just like oneself, created in the child's own image, and might therefore be used to complement the child in what he feels he lacks, as if the child and the imaginary friend were two halves of one person (which indeed they are!). Thus a child might imagine a twin as an addition to himself in order to overcome a sense of inferiority. A characteristic of an imaginary twin is that it provides an illusion of great strength and invincibility, the two combining to provide double strength. This is also a device used by actual twins!

Optimally, the child gradually recognises the split in himself and the way he is represented in the imaginary twin. The twinship then provides an opportunity for the child to weather the current difficulty and re-integrate the imaginary twin into himself as he becomes more able to tolerate the distress of his situation. Then the twinship fulfils its transitional function, and the child grows out of the need for his twin, without having to reject or disown it. However, where the hated aspects of the self are split off and projected into the imaginary friend and disowned in the longer term, the process may have a more damaging effect on development unless the split is later re-integrated into the self.

Thus, the imaginary friend of childhood may be variously used to gratify a longing for an object, as a temporary mechanism dealing with an unbearable situation or loss, to maintain omnipotent control of an object, or to avoid an external object relationship altogether.

CHAPTER TWO

Twins together: inter-twin dynamics

V ery frequently the first question asked when seeing or talking about twin babies is, "Are they identical?" This happens even if the babies are of different sexes. We seem to have an urgent longing to create a fantasy of identical twinship. In large part this will originate in our own early phantasy twin, as described in Chapter One. The vision of twins is also imbued with the strangeness of seeing what appears to be doubles, as I will discuss in Chapter Six. This common perception of twins as necessarily identical will have profound effects on the actual twins as they grow and develop. I will look at the intense necessity to understand that twins are individuals in their own right, with a particular and special bond between them.

This confusion has been well portrayed in the literature on twins:

> The layering, the intertwining. When someone looked at her and saw me. (Niffenegger, 2009, p. 371)

But as Penelope Farmer, herself a twin, writes:

> … identical twinship in particular confounds the sense that each person is unique … longing … for the myth of perfect companionship and understanding which reveals itself particularly in the

myth of twin souls; a condition for which twins are the paradigm
and so deeply envied—erroneously. (Farmer, 1996, pp. 5–6)

A child who is a twin has a different experience of the environment
from before birth compared with that of a child who is not a twin. Twins
will experience the same phase of development simultaneously. They
are in close physical and emotional proximity with another child born
to the same mother, throughout their development. For other siblings,
the differing sequences in birth and development and the differences
in status that develop within the family, enable each child to find an
individual path of development within the family context. Thus twins
are siblings of a particular kind. While they share many of the aspects
of other sibling relationships—the rivalry, love, companionship, peer
group support or pressure—there are other dynamics that make the
twin relationship unique amongst sibling relationships.

These particular qualities of the twin relationship are the result of a
number of factors.

As I have already described, twinning processes play a prominent
and distinctive role in the development of actual twins. The presence of a
twin, whatever the zygosity, same or opposite sex, offers the opportunity
for twinning phantasies to become concretised—for the phantasy twin
of infancy to be projected into the other twin, where it is then assumed
to reside. The other twin will be seen as the embodiment of the idealised
phantasy twin, as the ideal twin soul who will alleviate loneliness, be a
perfect companion, provide perfect understanding, and become a part of
the self that cannot be given up. Alternately the other twin may come to
represent the split off, unwanted aspects of the self. This concretisation
of a phantasy is likely become a permanent feature in the personalities
of the twins, to a greater or lesser degree. It is one of the factors that lead
to twins' experience of intense closeness or, alternatively, a vehement
insistence on their total separateness in their struggle to establish their
individuality—united in love or hate. The relationship between twins
has a profound and enduring effect on the development of a sense of self
in each twin, but it is important to note that pathological development
in twins is not necessarily attributable to the twinship *per se*.

The chronological age of the twins is almost identical, though it is
common for twins to make much of who was born first, whom is older
or younger, of the 10 minutes or half an hour between their births.
Different motivations may be involved in this, including competitive-
ness between the twins, the wish to differentiate and identify themselves

as separate and unique, and the wish to carve out some personal space in the twin relationship. This need for separateness runs alongside their wish to maintain aspects of the twinship that offer a sense of security, solidarity, and strength in numbers. In more problematic situations, this clinging to the twinship may lead to a sense of a joint or shared identity—a "we-self" instead of an "I".

The fact of virtually identical age has physical, physiological, psychological, and emotional consequences for each of the twins in their development. For each twin, the other twin will be ever-present in the minds of mother and father, and in the minds of each of the twins themselves. Mother's attention can never be wholly focused on one baby as she also always has another baby in mind. This may affect the development of the relationships between the babies and the mother, and between the twin babies themselves, as I discuss below.

There will obviously be practical factors to do with the individual care of each infant. For parents of twins there will always be a juggling of attention as the needs of each baby are taken into account at any one time. Inevitably attention given to one same-age infant at one moment will affect the amount and/or quality of attention given to the other. This is more potent for same-age children than those of different ages. Alessandro Piontelli suggested in 2002 that each infant is highly attuned to the level of age-appropriate attention offered, especially from the mother or primary caregiver. Observations indicate that the infant's jealousy and disturbance at not having mother's exclusive attention is more acute when the rival is of the same age, and more tolerable when the other child is a toddler or of a different age and requiring a different sort of attention. As Sigmund Freud said in 1916, "A child's demands for love are immoderate, they make exclusive claims and tolerate no sharing." (1916–1917, p. 334)

In observations of mothers of twins we often find her feeding one baby while engaging in social activity with the other twin—perhaps to compensate the other twin who is not at the breast. The attention given to each baby is in short bursts as mother's attention oscillates from one twin to the other. Sometimes the mother initially chooses to focus more on one twin than the other one, and this may become a long-lasting pattern. The reasons for the choice are often unconscious and may be based on a variety of factors which may include focusing on the weaker and smaller twin, the more active one, or one with particular physical features.

Twins create strategies to get more attention from mother and to impress on her and others that they too have needs and rights. This may include being more vocal than the other twin, whether with crying or talk-noises. They will clearly make it known when they feel left out. They are intensely watchful of the relationship between mother and the other twin.

The twinship

For all infants, developmental figures exist in two dimensions: the primary relationship with mother (and father) is the vertical dimension, while siblings offer a horizontal dimension and play a significant role in helping the individual to negotiate and manage peer social relationships. In fact, as Juliet Mitchell suggested in 2003, the existence of siblings propels us into having to confront issues that are not encountered in the parent–child relationship. On the other hand, peer relationships may be used to avoid being conscious of some of the frustrations and anxieties of being dependent on the parents/carers.

This brings us to an important understanding: in twins, the horizontal relationship with the other twin is highly significant and with its close unconscious emotional psychic and biological resonances, it may also be regarded as a primary relationship. As a result, it is not uncommon to find twins who are locked into an enmeshed relationship with each other, in a rigid structure that results in the impairment of individual development of each twin. Even where there has been a greater degree of individual personality development in each twin, and a sense of separate identity in each, there will always be a shadow of the other twin deep in the psyche of each.

The interaction of the internal twinning and external factors in the relationships between twins and their carers will create in twins an indelible internal twinship that will affect all relationships that each twin encounters, and will be a central part of their identities. It often remains unrecognised and may cause real difficulties in intimate relationships such as marriage, where the other partner comes to be regarded and related to as a "twin".

Twinning as a narcissistic state of mind

It is important in considering twin relationships to distinguish between the two aspects of the twin relationship. There are the "special" aspects of the relationship between twins like the unparalleled closeness and companionship of the twins. But there are also the more narcissistic elements of the twinship that may result in the idealisation of a twin relationship by twins and others where the twinship seems to exemplify and embody an understanding without words. In a companionable type of relationship, separateness and individuality can be achieved after the idealised phantasy twin is recognised for what it is and is relinquished and its loss mourned. Mourning for this lost ideal object is, however, never complete, hence our ubiquitous longing for perfect understanding.

Where the narcissistic aspects of the twin relationship predominate, the ideal twin-breast becomes concretely identified with the other twin. The ideal phantasy twin is not relinquished and the recognition of the loss of the longed-for perfect understanding is evaded. This may lead to an enmeshed twinship in which each twin feels dependent on the other twin for his identity, indeed for his survival; but it also creates a relationship in which the twins feel trapped, suffocated in a deadly tangle.

In a fused narcissistic twin relationship, the sense of self of each twin becomes so identified with the incorporated other twin, that the boundary between the self and the other twin, and of an identity separate from the other twin, may be denied. The twins may believe that the twinship offers them a sustaining system in which they are self-sufficient and that they have no need of any other objects. The enmeshed narcissistic twinship may then be used as a psychic retreat from development as an individual. The twinship refuge may offer apparent safety. The unbearable anxiety that is associated with development towards individuality and separateness for each twin within the twin relationship is avoided. However, alongside the apparent safety offered by the psychic retreat, the twins would feel trapped in the narcissistic twin relationship. Intense anxieties would accompany any attempt to emerge from this refuge from development. In the extreme these anxieties may be experienced as a sense of fragmentation of the self.

This sort of maladaptive twin relationship may emerge when there has not been enough attention and containment by the parents. The lack of containment may be the result of inadequate resources in an inherently difficult situation; of the emotional fragility of maternal and paternal care; or of inherent unmanageable anxieties in the twins themselves. Where the babies have difficulty tolerating frustration, they will seize on any avenue or opportunity to help them cope, and this may mean clinging to the other immature twin for a sense of security. Whatever the cause of this lack in development it would be a potent factor promoting the use of the twinship as a psychic retreat.

Questions have been raised as to whether the twin relationship is no more than a version of a narcissistic relationship, a narcissistic entanglement. This view does not take account of a major difference for twins—not only is there a phantasy merging with mother as a twin, as experienced by all infants, but in addition the twins have deep sensory, pre-verbal protomental experiences of each other from both intra-uterine and post-birth closeness. These experiences will create enduring memory traces that are somatic, or bodily, in their expression. Such sensate memory traces in each infant will be made up from heartbeat, movement, touching, pushing, smell, sounds. These unconscious memory traces are central to the indelible internal twinning that persists even in the most developed and evolved twin pairs. So the narcissistic phantasies of oneness in twins have a bodily base, the early pre-verbal memories both twins have of each other and mother, in addition to the early close encounter with mother. In contrast, for singletons the phantasies of merger and the longed-for narcissistic oneness are based solely on the early relationship with mother.

The dynamics and tensions in the twin relationship are more intense than those in other sibling relationships, and are of a different nature from those between children and their parents. The absence of an age gap between the twins creates an inter-twin dynamic based on both a longing for sameness and an intense need for differentiation. The twinship lacks the developmental advantages offered by the age difference between non-twin siblings, but the twin relationship does provide an opportunity for unparalleled companionship and for an understanding without words, reminiscent of the earliest relationship with mother. The twinship is also a relationship where intensified rivalry and competition become very active, and may thus also engender strong negative feelings towards each other.

The existence of a twin may even ameliorate developmental difficulties in situations of maternal unavailability or neglect. However, a sound "friendship" is not necessarily a feature of the twin relationship. Many factors will affect how the twin relationship develops, and the extent to which each twin within the relationship develops a companionable rather than an antagonistic or narcissistic relationship with the other twin. Siblings and others may envy the closeness of twins, and the twins may use the twinship to create a barrier around the twin pair, isolating themselves from the parents and other family members.

When twins inhabit a very enmeshed twin relationship, the idea of separateness between them and of actual separation of any kind may be experienced as life threatening. The twins are so heavily invested in and identified with each other that a move towards separateness would be experienced as a loss of an essential part of the self. Because of the narcissistic nature of the relationship, it would feel not just like dying, but also like annihilation. This is evident in the states of panic that are engendered when such separations and losses occur in twins (see Chapter Three).

As an example of such extreme entanglement in twins, I described in an earlier paper in 2002, the sad plight of the Gibbons twins described by Marjorie Wallace in 1996. June and Jennifer Gibbons were MZ twins who lived their lives isolated from their parents and siblings, and from the external world. From childhood, they shared a secret language and spoke only to one another, and to a younger sister. They would not allow their parents into their twin relationship, and it may be that in this displaced and isolated family, not much parental attention was available. At school the twins remained mute, frozen in their silence. As teenagers they became even more reclusive. They began to exhibit rather bizarre and delinquent behaviour and at seventeen they were both jailed for repeated arson and theft. In jail they were separated.

Wallace described her first interview with June while she was in prison:

> I could see June's eyes flickering and her mouth edging into something resembling a smile. But her words were torn whispers, her whole being was strung between a desperate need to speak and some destructive internal command which forbade her such freedom. She would start to tell me something, then suddenly gag as though an invisible presence had put its hands around her throat. Who or what could hold such power over a human being, to compel her to lifelong silence and immobility? What inner force gave her the strength to reject everything and everyone offering help or affection? What had happened to allow a potentially attractive young girl to waste her youth, not just behind the walls of a prison but behind her own private defences? (Wallace, 1996, p. 5)

It is as if June experienced her twin sister, Jennifer, as a highly restrictive internal presence that could not be challenged or overcome. They were utterly bound in a complex relationship of love and hate, with much emphasis on the murderous hatred between them. As Jennifer expressed in relation to June and the twinship: "She should have died at birth. Cain killed Abel. No twin should ever forget that." (Wallace, 1996, p. 140)

With equal tortured hatred, June wrote: "Nobody suffers the way I do. Not with a sister. With a husband—yes. With a wife—yes. With a child—yes. But this sister of mine, a dark shadow robbing me of sunlight, is my one and only torment." (Wallace, 1996, p. 167)

June expressed the mortal entanglement with and ambivalence between her and Jennifer rather graphically, in a poem: "Without my shadow would I die?/Without my shadow would I gain life?/*Be free or left to die?*" (Wallace, 1996, p. 255; my emphasis)

For all twin pairs, each twin has to struggle with his own processes of development to carve out a personal sense of identity within the twin relationship, which is fundamentally present for both of them. For each twin, the individuality established will overlap to varying degrees with the individuality of the other twin, creating common areas of a shared identity alongside the individual ones. These shared areas form the core of the twin relationship and the individual twins negotiate around it from their more individual centres.

The phantasy twin that originates from a deep unconscious understanding between mother and baby becomes the basis for the importance of the sense of comfort offered by the teddy bears, soft toys, special blankets, and sheets that young children cling to. The objects serve as comforters for this sense of longing, and are imbued with, and based upon, the original creation of a phantasy twin. Donald Winnicott wrote in 1953 about a "transitional object", that is an imagined object that bridges the gap between the baby and the longed-for mother. The imagined object is created by the infant as a link with mother, and it comes to be represented by an actual object such as soft toys and so on.

A transitional object will become irrelevant as the child grows beyond the need to find a substitute for mother and develops a capacity for symbolising, thinking, relating to others, and for being alone. The baby will relinquish the transitional object in order to pave the way for external relationships with others. Likewise, ordinarily the phantasy twin of infancy will fade as a more coherent sense of self develops, though its shadow lingers through life. For twins this may well be more complex. Where the actual twin has come to be seen as an embodiment of the phantasy twin and is ever present, the other twin may be used as a transitional object and may become a concretised representation of twin one. Development towards separate identities and a mature capacity for symbolisation will be compromised, as will each individual twin's capacity for relating to others in a mature way.

Thus the phantasy twin that originates in our imagination in our very earliest days, and the existence of an actual twin, together create a situation where the phantasy seems to have become a reality. The mechanism for this is: we project our phantasy of an internal twin onto the external twin who is so ever-present, and the actual external twin becomes an embodiment of the imagined phantasy twin. It is inevitable for twins, given the very early primitive nature of the processes and the phantasy twin, that the mutually internalised twin will become a long-term internal psychic arrangement for each twin, to a greater or lesser degree. This has profound importance for psychic development of each of the twins, and for the development of a sense of self.

A phantasy twin differs greatly from an actual twin. The phantasy twin is a creation by the infant that it controls omnipotently. The actual twin is not controlled in this way and, most importantly, is not just an expression or extension of the individual's personality. The conflicts and rivalry between actual twins complicate the closeness that is so longed for in a phantasy twin. Each twin will develop within the twinship with his own phantasy of an ideal twin, which will be projected onto the other twin. The phantasy of having a twin that emanates from each of the twins themselves as well as in the perceptions of others plays a prominent role in reinforcing the actual twinship. Thus there will be intra- and inter-psychic factors affecting the twin relationship, and factors external to the twinship linked with the perceptions of the twin pair by others. The external and internal factors interact to create an enduring and binding twinship. We can therefore see that there is a vast difference between wishing for a twin and having an actual twin.

It is important that twins should be seen and treated as two individuals within a relationship, rather than as clones of each other. Twins face many pressures in their lives to be a pair rather than two distinct individuals. These expectations emanate from society, parents, and of course from the internal twinning processes. While the twin relationship represents the at-oneness and emotional closeness we all long for, it has powerful tensions within it, and the twins will feel threatened by the development of maturational separateness. Twins are regarded as special because of the nature of the relationship they share and what it means for all of us, and it is difficult for them to relinquish this state of apparent at-oneness and the celebrity that accompanies it.

Development and genetic factors

A great deal of research has been carried out based on the assumption that MZ twins are genetically identical. Genes are the blueprint from which our development takes instruction, but they are rarely the singular factor that determines which way our development progresses or is altered, and they are not immutable. There have been many new developments in this field and our understanding of how genes work has increased enormously.

The use of twins to try to establish whether nature or nurture—that is, genetics or environment—is the greater contributory factor in development in a specific area, has a long history. But twin research has increasingly been shown to be flawed except in very specific areas of inherited diseases. Ideas that specific behaviours are caused by a particular gene are largely fallacious and are based on misleading and flawed research. Genes are complex, multi-faceted, and changeable. They operate as multiple units influenced by many factors and they may mutate as a result of environmental pressures.

Jay Joseph addresses twin research and genetics in depth in his book *The Gene Illusion* (2004). He examines, amongst other things, the much-reported research since the 1950s on cases of MZ twins separated at birth and apparently brought up in different environments. He questions the research findings that conclude that these separated twins appear to make the same life choices in a way that seems extraordinary and uncanny. In these research findings, reunited twins are reported to have the same taste and lifestyle, even marry someone with the same name, or choose identical clothes, simply because of their genetic similarity. Joseph examines these studies and concludes from his extensive research that genes per se cannot determine how so-called "identical" twins develop, whether they have been reared apart or together. He asserts that the research into twins separated at birth has not taken into account many factors that were formative in creating the apparent similarities that were so heralded, thus skewing the findings.

Joseph found that much of the research on twins reared apart was flawed or inadequate. For example, he notes that a pair of twins reported that they had both lied to the researchers, to fuel the "we are the same" myth; that some of the twins had had many years of contact after the initial separation; that some twins were only partially separated in early life and they did have meaningful contact while growing up; and that it was useful for them to exaggerate what they had in common because of the attention it generated. The researchers stress what the twins have in common, but not what sets them apart, nor what part coincidence might have played in the similarities discovered. In other words, the researchers have selected which facts they present to the world as twin research in order to feed the myth about twins and genetic identicality. In other words, there is a bias in favour of similarity in much of the research and much of the critical research has been dismissed.

Joseph focuses on the theory and methodology of twin research from Frances Galton to the current day. Most notorious of the researchers was Josef Mengele in Auschwitz, where he conducted experiments on about 3,000 sets of twins—only 200 were alive after the war. This "most active and influential" (Joseph, 2004, p. 43) twin researcher experimented on and murdered twins in the name of science, using the co-twin research method. There are, understandably, deep concerns about using any of his findings.

Another aspect of concern in these studies is the methods used in the assessment of the environment and how it may influence development. It is often stated that the environment for children growing up together is the same—same parents, same home with all its comforts, discomforts, and idiosyncrasies. As any siblings or twins, whether MZ or DZ will testify, this is patently not so. Each child will have its own individual experience of its relationships with its parents, with other siblings, and the environment. So we must conclude that twins do not share either identical genes or the same environment.

A large research project started in Minnesota has received a considerable amount of press and media attention and excitement, but there are queries about these findings too. Jay Joseph (2004) concluded that the Minnesota studies of twins reared apart were unreliable. The life histories and test scores have not been made available for independent inspection. The importance of the environmental similarity for the twins has been overlooked. Furthermore these twins were recruited on the basis of their similarity and their pre-existing knowledge of each other. Such criticism has been dismissed and the reports offer only selected and incomplete data. Thus we must conclude that the research on twins supposedly reared apart tell us little about the genetic influence on the various psychological trait differences, on IQ, or any other factors other than specific genetically based diseases.

We all have a set of given genes at conception, but the operation of these genes is both varied and complex. Each gene has a number of versions of itself that can be activated or de-activated by other factors, so the behaviour of genes varies according to the conditions the foetus finds itself in. Thus, even MZ twin foetuses from a single fertilised egg, with initially identical genomes (the complete set of genes or genetic material present in a cell or organism), will differ in how their genes behave and affect their development.

Our development depends on how our genes are activated and expressed. Recent research has shown that identical genes can diverge in their expression both during foetal development and during the course of a lifetime, as a result of so-called "epigenetic" factors. "Epigenomes" are basically chemical switches that activate or deactivate the particular genes, which then lay the template for the formation of proteins—the building blocks for development of all kinds.

Epigenetics forms the new focus of understanding for how we become whom we are. It offers an explanation of how our genes will be activated or deactivated, and altered from conception and through life, by the various chemical, hormonal and environmental factors we encounter, and will affect how we develop and who we become. Most genes act as multiples working together, and there are different versions of genes that become activated or deactivated. Very few genes provide the single determining factor in development.

As already mentioned in the introduction, epigenetics is the missing third element between genes and environmental. Tim Spector describes, in his book *Identically Different* (2012), how despite having similar genetic patterns, epigenetics affects the behaviour of genes in a way such that even MZ twins become different as they develop.

Any theory that oversimplifies the factors in development, like the rather rigid debate about genes versus environment, is bound to leave us without a full understanding of how we develop. All organisms, particularly the higher order ones, are extremely complex, and are formed by an interacting network of cells, their genes, the particular expression of the genes, and the way they work together. This complex interaction is orchestrated in a way that is flexible and responsive to other factors and pressures. It is not rigid or predetermined.

Current research indicates that genes and our genetic destiny can be changed. Our genome is not a given for life. Even one-time environmental life events can implant a lifelong genetic memory within the cells and these changes can be inherited by the children of parents and grandparents who have experienced those events. In other words, you can change your genes, your genetic destiny, and that of your children and grandchildren through environmental experiences.

Thus epigenetic factors will create differences between all twins with consequent changes in their developmental patterns. As a result of the action of epigenetic factors, the categorisation of twins as "identical" and "fraternal" no longer holds the certainty of information that was previously thought. It has created much greater ambiguity in our classification of types of twins, and what we might understand about their genetic similarities and differences, and their development.

Factors like health, personality, taste, and appearance all depend on both nature and nurture, with epigenetics as the link between the two. Nutrition, space, exposure to hormones, small alterations in epigenetic profile, and minute differences in the genome—all these factors create subtle but important differences in each twin. Genes do not create specific physical or mental attributes, or personality traits per se. Genes and the environment, both intrauterine and after birth, will affect all our development. Whether singletons, twins, or other multiples, personal individual factors will shape our responses to, and our manner of dealing with, the situations we encounter, as we build an individual and unique identity.

These important factors in development leave me wondering about the status of the research being undertaken by the space agency, NASA. MZ twins Scott and Mark Kelly are both astronauts. Nasa is going to conduct an experiment in which Scott will be in the international space station for a year while Mark will remain on earth as a control. They are hoping to learn about the effects of a prolonged period in space, and will try to assess the effects of stressors like radiation, weightlessness, confinement, and monotony. Nasa scientists will study molecular, physiological, psychological, and microbiological subtle changes in both men and compare them and the effects that space travel has on the genes. They claim the study will offer clues that can be followed up by other research. Given that their genes are not identical to start with, that changes in genes are multifactorial, and that psychology is never based simply on genetic make-up, this research (based on the idea that MZ twins have identical genes) seems to be flawed from the start. Is Mark Kelly really a control for Scott?

In contrast, I recently came across the triumph of common sense over the pressures to maintain a belief that twins are identical, on the High Street:

> A mother with twins (blond, blue eyes) pushed a double buggy up the road. An elderly woman leaned over the babies, ooh-ing and aah-ing and asked, "Are they twins?"
>
> Mother, "Yes"
>
> Elderly woman, "Aren't they lovely! Why don't you dress them alike? They look so cute."
>
> Mother, irritated/bemused, replied, "But they are not the same person."

Bravo mother! She does have MZ twins that look alike, but as she has so clearly recognised, they are not the same person, and they do not share a personality. Each baby is an individual in its own right as well as being a member of a pair of twins. She has avoided the tendency to try and amalgamate twins, especially cute little ones.

The developmental framework

When I met with a group of mothers of twins, I learned that many of them felt guilty that they had not been able to give optimal attention to each of the twin babies. They imagined that if they had had just one baby, they would have had a perfect mother–baby experience. Instead of this, they felt they were constantly juggling their attention between the babies, and somehow short-changing them both.

Of course, as any mother of a single baby knows, there is no such thing as a perfect mother–baby relationship. There are good times and difficult times. Sometimes the baby is fractious, cries for no apparent reason, is inconsolable, and so on. Sometimes the mother is too tired, distressed, or depressed to offer the baby as much as she would like. So the ideal of being a perfect mother that many mothers of twins have, a standard of which they believe they are falling short, is a fallacy and may have a deeper source. However, there are realities in that having to divide their attention between two babies of the same age will affect the intimate relationship with each baby and will have developmental consequences.

The developmental picture for twins is inevitably more complex than for a single baby. Each twin would have unique experiences in her relationships both with mother and with the other twin. Research has shown that the interaction between mother and each infant would stimulate the brain development of the baby and will affect the socio-emotional development of each child. The relationship with the other twin would have a different effect but would again be unique to each twin. In addition each twin would have her personal perception of both her own and her twin's relationship with mother. Each twin would therefore develop differentially according to her unique experience with mother and with her twin.

The very early relationship with mother will occur at an unconscious, preverbal level, and will include the mother's awareness and unconscious understanding of her babies' needs, the emotional contact between them, and the physical attention she gives to each of the babies and the nature of it. The twinship will exert a different pressure on both the individual development of each twin and the development of the twinship. It will also affect the development of the relationship of each twin with mother, again at preverbal levels. The relationship between the twins will be exclusive to them. As Penelope Farmer describes: "whereas a single child relates at the start only to its mother, twins right from birth, and even before, have a relationship to which neither parent has any access" (1996, p. 12).

In Chapter One, I described the ways in which the mother regulates her infant's emotional states, and this has been confirmed by studies of neurological resonances. For all twins, the infants would share a biological responsiveness to each other based on their closeness in utero—their movements, heartbeats, and so on, and this will be an additional factor in the emotional regulation of both babies. In MZ twins, this would be particularly linked with the similar programming of their nervous systems, given the similarity in their genetic make-up, as well as their closeness in utero, sometimes even sharing a placenta and amniotic sac. According to Alan Schore (in a personal communication) MZ twins would share similar brain and body rhythms to an extent greater than most other individuals. This factor will complicate the regulation of emotions between the twins and between infants and mother.

Thus MZ twins in particular would resonate psycho-biologically. The state of arousal they experience would be amplified rather than reduced by the arousal of the other twin because the frequency of

the external sensory stimulation would coincide with their genetically encoded intrinsic rhythms. This would have an impact on their
attempts at attachment and separation and on their development, as we
see in some twin pairs.

Through the interaction between twins both in utero and after birth,
they will, to varying degrees, affect the regulation of emotional states
for each other. Where the mother is not fully available to regulate her
babies' emotions, each baby's state of arousal would not be properly
modulated and the babies may be left overly aroused which if not
managed will impede their development. For the twins regulating each
other, the effect would be that one immature infant would regulate
another equally immature one and this would be likely to escalate the
levels of arousal rather than modulate them, creating developmental
difficulties.

Intrauterine experience and differential development in twins

The constant dynamic and developmental changes in the intra-uterine
environment would not only modify behavioural development of
each foetus, but may also be modified by the foetus. Seventy per cent
of MZ twins are mono-chorionic (share a placenta) and di-amniotic
(MC-DA). Thirty per cent of MZ twins are di-chorionic and di-amniotic
(DC-DA). And a very small percentage of MZ twins share a common
placenta and amniotic sac. Even in this situation, the placenta is not
equally shared, and the amniotic fluid is not equally distributed
between them.

There have been a few cases in which a woman with two wombs
(a condition known as "didelphys") has carried twins, one in each
womb. In this situation, there will be less interaction between the twins
due to thickness of the wall of the womb, though there would still be
some awareness of presence of other twin, as they would hear each
other's heartbeats, and vie for space as they developed.

There has also been a case reported where a woman with two wombs
carried two babies that were conceived a week apart. So they would not
technically be twins, but would share the same difficulties that twins
encounter. (Hough & Thompson, 2013)

We have looked at the genetic and epigenetic factors, our inheritance,
and what they mean for our development. Now I will consider individual developmental aspects.

Just as MZ twins are never genetically identical, they are never tem-
peramentally or behaviourally identical though they may show similar
mannerisms. MZ twins have different levels of activity in utero and by
twenty to twenty-two weeks we find the same level of discrepancy in
their behavioural activity as we see between DZ twins. The basis for
future behavioural development is laid down in prenatal life and the
separate experiences of prenatal life engender behavioural differences
in both MZ and DZ twins. No individual emerges from the prenatal
period as an identical copy of someone else. All are quite different and
unique. Prenatal factors are more evident than genetic inheritance and
traits noted in each twin in utero continue after birth.

Along with the individual differences observed between twins
in utero, the patterns of interaction between twins whether, MZ or
DZ, persist after birth, as they relate to the personality of the infant
(Alessandra Piontelli, 2002). It is not clear at what stage of development
the infants have sufficient neural development to recognise and perceive the other twin as a twin sibling, but it is clear that the interaction
between them from before birth has an impact on their development
and relationship.

In utero, foetuses are responsive to touch and have an unconscious
perception of movement and spatial orientation arising from stimuli
within their own bodies. For twins, contact with, and development of
awareness of, each other will vary. Up to ten to twelve weeks, only MZ
twins sharing a placenta (mono-chorionic) may stimulate each other
because there is no membrane between them. Most MZ twins will have
a thin membrane between them and share a placenta so some contact between them is possible. DZ twins may have some contact from
thirteen weeks. All twins from fifteen weeks can have intra-pair stimulation though they are not always responsive to each other—they show
periods of sensory-motor inhibition.

Activity in foetuses is often equated with wakefulness and therefore with intentionality and consciousness. In reality the behaviourally
active foetus is not awake but in a different phase of sleep. It has brief
episodes of wakefulness only when close to full term. When they are
active, one twin foetus may impinge on the other, but the other may
remain unresponsive. The foetus may feel and sense stimulation from
the other twin but we should not attach interpretations to these sensa-
tions and instil them with meaning. While there is likely to be some
sensate memory of such events, they will not carry the sort of memory

constructs we encounter later in their development. They will, however, leave an enduring sensate memory trace that is so evident and important in the twin relationship.

There is much research on the early stages of foetal development (see Chamberlain, 2013; Anand & Hickey, 1987; Hartmann & Zimberoff, 2002). The senses develop early in utero. Foetuses respond to touch from eight weeks after conception, the sensitive areas increasing gradually until at thirty-two weeks, nearly all parts of the body are sensitive to a light stroke of a single hair. Pain perception exists from the seventh week after conception as shown by effects on the cardio-respiratory system, hormonal and metabolic changes, motor response, facial expressions, and crying. From six to ten weeks, foetuses become physically active, stretch, and move their heads and limbs. Patterns of movement have been observed at twenty weeks. This movement is spontaneous, internally generated, and we see cycles between activity and rest. Foetuses make breathing movements and jaw movements. They use their hands to interact with other parts of the body and with the umbilical cord. This early movement may be spontaneous or may be provoked by stimuli from the environment. Tasting begins at about fourteen weeks, and smell at about the same time. Hearing and listening reactively begins at sixteen weeks. They respond to light at twenty-six weeks as seen in body movements and heart rate.

Foetuses exhibit predictable patterns of behaviour at thirty-six weeks, representing integration between various centres on the central nervous system. Memory for prenatal experiences such as the sound of mother's voice, songs, and lullabies, particular stories mother reads to them before they are born, are present from birth. From twenty-six weeks the intonation, rhythms, speech patterns of mother's voice are recognised. The foetus has already learned the neural patterns of language, including the emotional context in utero.

From about thirty-two weeks, babies in utero can focus visually and track horizontally and vertically. Researchers even suggest that babies start dreaming as early as twenty-three weeks, as observed by their rapid eye movements. Intense dream activity in premature babies can occur at thirty weeks. It diminishes as the infant shifts from one hundred per cent sleep time in premature babies to fifty per cent sleep by term. During dreams the foetus is active, involving apparently coherent movements of the face and limbs in synchrony with the dream itself. The foetus exhibits pleasant or unpleasant expressions. Dreaming is also an internally generated activity. It is neither reactive nor evoked, but instead expresses inner mental or emotional experiences. However, the newborn baby has no sense of self or identity until he develops this over time within the context of his relationship with mother and significant others in his life.

Given the sensitivity and awareness at some level of developing babies in utero, it is inevitable that the twins will interact with, and in many ways be aware of, each other at some level. Initially, when they are still very small, there will not really be any significant impact on each other, though for a mother who knows she is pregnant with twins, she will have two babies in mind from very early on in the pregnancy. We don't know what of her expectations is transmitted to the twins in utero, but most certainly after birth this will become an issue, as Alessandro Piontelli (2002) has so well documented.

In utero, twins exhibit synchrony in sleep and awake states, in movement, heart rate accelerations, and blood pressure as a result of their shared environment and mutual tactile communication (Nyqvist, 1998). After birth, differences between them become apparent in their activity, irritability, and resistance to soothing and sleep patterns. Research indicates that co-bedding twins after birth was supportive to them in the transition from intra-uterine to extra-uterine life. Twins were observed moving closer to each other, touching, holding, hugging, and waking at the same time. The intra-uterine sensate experiences each twin will have of the other twin will create sensate memories and expectations about what feels natural after birth. Continued close physical contact in newly born twins, especially premature ones, may help them adjust to post-uterine life.

Twins may not react to each other from the start though research on co-bedding, especially with premature twins, shows their awareness of the proximity of the other baby and the comfort and support that this may offer. It is likely that the comforting aspect of having the other twin close by is based on the sense of presence of the other twin with his familiar resonances. The absence of the other baby might be felt as the loss of an expected presence. So the sense of comfort in the presence of the other baby would depend on expectations based on experience rather than on affect regulation.

It is important to re-state that the very early uterine experiences and memories of the other twin sharing the womb would be pre-verbal, pre-symbolic, sensate memories. As such, they would be visceral in nature, remembered bodily rather than through verbal or visual pictures.

We see this kind of memory at times in relationships when there is a sense of merging, like falling in love. But we also find this experience of a bodily-remembered memory where someone has suffered a traumatic experience that cannot be processed by ordinary mental means, and where it remains as a visceral, overwhelming memory.

Thus each twin arrives in the world with someone from the womb, someone with whom it has been interacting at some level, in a way that will create just such sensate primitive memories. So there will always be an area of relating between twins that exists on this preverbal, sensate, visceral level, and this will be a central factor in the indelible twin bond. At some level, they will feel as if they are bound together by forces out of their control, unconscious processes holding them in relation to each other on a visceral level. This sense of bonding from a prenatal state will create a powerful tension in the twins. After birth they will be aware of the other body that was there with them in the womb with its own particular rhythms.

After birth, we can observe infants arousing each other. One awakens and cries, wakes the other, and both become more and more disturbed and desperate until they have been attended to. Attention to the needs of babies is sometimes hindered because the parents do not yet understand what is leading to the baby's discomfort. Recently, consultant Gillian Kennedy, speech therapist at University College Hospital London, was honoured for her work with neonates—she specialises in working with non-verbal communication with vulnerable new infants in order to enable appropriate connections to develop in the brain. She observes and interprets a range of non-verbal signs in babies—their breathing or particular jerky limb movements—to help staff and parents respond to the baby's particular health needs. As with the emotionally attuned mother, this level of understanding will have an impact on the baby's mental and emotional development.

As an example of problematic development of twins consequent upon a lack of individual development, Dorothy Burlingham, in 1963, observed twins Bill and Bert. These twin brothers stirred each other to ever-greater peaks of excitement and loss of control throughout much of their lives. They suffered considerable parental neglect in their early days and eventually grew up in the Hampstead Nurseries. Bert and Bill were so alike that it was difficult for mother and the staff who dealt with them to tell them apart. They were frequently mistaken for each other and were often called Billybert or Bertbilly. When they were separated as infants, each would mistake his image in a mirror for his twin. They were indeed mirror images of each other in posture and in movement. They were intensely competitive throughout their lives and the jealousy and rivalry between them could be quite murderous. This extended into their teens, and when they were in therapy at a time when they were beginning to establish some sense of separateness.

Bill and Bert constantly sought excitement and seemed to have no empathy for any other children, hurting others without any sense of guilt or shame. They developed a way of being with each other by adopting complementary abilities as a means of coping with their rivalry. They felt both murderous towards each other, and also totally absorbed with each other. Like the Gibbons twins referred to before, they did not relate to anyone outside the twinship, but they attacked each other repeatedly. Sometimes they acted together as a gang of two, and attacked a group of children at the school.

This narcissistic identification with each other diminished gradually when each twin realised that the other twin was a separate person, not merely a duplication of himself. Their earlier enmeshed identification with each other had finally changed to a situation in which they could allow themselves to be different from the other twin. They discovered they could safely allow some separateness between them, and that they did need not continually to react in identical ways that resulted in a lack of individuation. Their wishes, needs, impulses as their own person were enhanced. They recognised the other twin was both a rival as well as a twin to each other, each with their own needs for attention and satisfaction. Thus what had been a crippling and limiting twinship gradually gave way to a somewhat more balanced relationship between the twins, of individuals in a twin relationship.

Language development in twins

It is often assumed that language development in twins is delayed because of the fact that they are twins, but this is not inevitable. There are various factors that will affect the acquisition or impediment of language in twins, including the background, the quality of parental care, and the amount of attention given to each twin. One factor may be that twins use each other as language models, and mimic each other's immature speech in their attempt to communicate. However, while twins may give the appearance that they actually understand each other's babbling, initially they are really just experimenting with sounds and words. The inter-twin babble would create a degree of unintelligibility in their speech. As all babies do, twins practise the vocalisation that establishes connections in their brain and that lead to language development.

The quality of pre-linguistic interaction between mother and each of her twins is likely to differ from that of a mother with her single baby. This difference may affect language development in twins and may result in an initial delay in language acquisition. Where this does occur, twins usually catch up with single children by about three years. In a study by Sue Butler, Catherine McMahon, and Judy Ungerer in 2002, mothers of twins were found to be less focused on their twin infants, and less responsive to the infants' non-vocal cues. The mothers did not regard the infant communications as particularly informative and deliberate, when compared with mothers of single infants. The language-learning environment for twins often differed from that for singletons.

Mothers of twins have less opportunity to learn the meanings of their young infants' more subtle behavioural cues. The observed differences in language delay in twins were noted to be greater in situations in which mother needed to understand and interpret the infant's internal states from the baby's noises and non-verbal communications. A mother of twins will have less time to spend individually with her infants in focused dyadic interactions, where there are two infants to interact with, and she has less time to develop a unique language with each of them. In addition, the style of speech used by mothers of twins may also be influenced by her concern about the wellbeing of the other twin. The lag in language development for twins is about three months, once overt handicaps as a result of early birth or perinatal issues have been taken into account.

For older twins, an often-mentioned aspect of language development is the idea that they share a secret language, a form of communication known only to them. This is usually referred to as idioglossia (idiosyncratic language) or cryptophasia (twin talk). Twins can develop the ability to communicate with one another without working within the grammar of their parents' language. Usually the twins are closely attuned to minute signs or sounds between them and use this to communicate with each other. It is more rare that they speak a true twin language. Where there is a private language between twins, it consists mostly of distortions of ordinary words. Some twins will develop some form of unique language, using nicknames, gestures, abbreviations, or terminology that they only use with each other. While parents and siblings can often discern the meaning, the twins generally don't use these terms with others. This close communication between twins may be another factor that contributes to the short-term delay in linguistic development of one or both twins.

It is important to distinguish between shared verbal understanding, i.e. children's talk that is understandable to them but not to others, but where the talk is not focused exclusively on the other twin; and a private language in which communication is directed exclusively towards the other twin. Thorpe, Greenwood, Eivers, and Rutter (2001) found these two kinds of communication were common to all children, not only twins, up to the age of twenty months. Both these kinds of communication decline between twenty to thirty-six months as better language patterns of communication develop. Shared verbal understanding is twice as common in twins as compared with other siblings in the second year of life, when verbal ability is less developed. By thirty-six months, only twins continue to use a private language. But even between twins, the use of a private language becomes very uncommon after this time.

The persistence of private forms of communication after three years of age is indicative of a greater level of closeness and dependency between the twins. However it is not clear whether the closeness between the twins predates the development of the private language, or is a consequence of it. Where a private language does persist, it is usually accompanied by language impairment, but again this impairment may be the precursor to the private language. The private language usually disappears by six years.

In a comprehensive review of the literature on language development in twins in 1992, Elizabeth Bryan noted that in one study, it is observed that twins pass through the stages of speech development in a way that is different from singletons. They have a much more complicated inter-action to deal with, as they have to learn early how to communicate within a triad, and when to engage and disengage in discourse. There are always two recipients and two responders to any communication within the triad. She proposes that this may postpone other aspects of language acquisition. Bryan stresses the importance of early intervention where there are difficulties, but notes that speech delay in twins is neither inevitable nor irremediable.

In addition to environmental factors relating to the amount of time and attention available, which will influence the development of language, twins are more likely to suffer perinatal problems that may delay acquisition of speech. The acquisition of speech is a highly complex process and it is heavily dependent on the personal interaction between mothers and babies and between the twins themselves—the interaction between the twins will also slow the learning of speech patterns.

Thus, there will inevitably be more difficulty on both sides of the equation for twins and mothers of twins. Mother has to bear two babies in mind, even when one is asleep, or not in the same room. She has to prepare for and relate to them both when she herself is under much greater stress than if she had only one baby. At night, she will be lucky to have a few hours' sleep, and mothers of twins complain of being constantly tired. For the twins, they will not have the same attention as a single baby would and they may well turn to each other for comfort as well as company, but as immature "containers", this too may create problems for them.

The development of the twinship and individual identity

Twins exist both as individuals and as members of a particular dyad. It is essential for their emotional health that each is enabled to develop a sense of a personal identity as well as that of a twin. The personal identity will develop within the context of the twinship, and the relationship with mother and father and others in their lives. The sense of self as a discrete person with one's own needs, beliefs, abilities, and personal history, all connected in a dynamic ever-changing internal structure, enables us to have a personal identity. In addition to other factors, the experience of being a twin will form an integral and enduring part of that personal structure.

We might think of the sense of self as gradually building within a psychic membrane or skin until an individual has a more or less coherent idea that "this is me". This process is more complex for twins. As with all children, the sense of self develops within the intimate relationship with mother and father. For a twin there is always another twin present actually and in the minds of both infant and parents. The sense of identity both within and outside the twinship will have to accommodate some overlap between the twins in which the sense of self is to a greater or lesser extent shared, or the boundaries between them less clear.

The creation of a sense of identity will depend of factors such as the way of seeing oneself in relation to the world as a separate and discrete individual, and in relation to one's body. Personal boundaries and the development of an identity separate from others are an essential part of individuality. For twins, their perceptions of similarities between them are more important than their zygosity as they struggle towards individuality. Factors in the environment and within the twin unit itself will influence the extent to which each twin develops as an individual or alternately suffers fused and confused concepts of the self. And each twin will experience this differently and achieve different levels of maturity.

There will be powerful dynamic processes between the twins in which they identify with each other and project into each other both the idealised phantasy twin and the hated and disowned aspects of the self. These twinning processes are part of the development of all babies, but because of the lack of age differentiation between twins and the early sensate experiences each twin has of the other twin, the twinning processes have a particular nature. The twin-twin identification will be more powerful and embodied that it would for other siblings. The sense of self and other will probably be more blurred, and in the extreme may even be fused.

The degree of twinning between twins, enhanced by factors like the parental and societal attitudes, will affect the development of a sense of a separate identity. The greater the twinning between twins, the less the sense of personal identity each twin will develop, and the more likely it is that they will remain enmeshed in the twin relationship at the cost of personal identity.

Separateness and separation from the other twin are central to the development of each twin. This does not mean that separation leads to the ending of the twinship. The twin relationship is an enduring, indeed a valuable and an ineradicable, relationship. It is necessary to enable each twin to find separateness and individuality within the twin relationship without either denying the importance of the twinship or psychically murdering the other twin. We could view this development as the twin relationship changing from a more narcissistic twinship to a twin relationship that is more mature and tolerant of difference and of relationships with others.

Compared with singletons, twins have two primary emotional ties, the twinship and the relationship with mother (and later father). These relationships exist simultaneously and will influence each other, and may also act against each other. Twins thus have a dual task: first, that of dealing with their conflicting feelings of love and hate within both the relationship with mother and with the twin; and second, they will have to find a balance between the two sets of relationships. Even when separated from the other twin and alone with mother, the experience may not to be as straightforward or pleasurable as expected, as the wish for sole possession of mother is too strong and leads to a too great awareness of the absent rival for her attention and love.

Separation from mother can cause great distress, as all parents have witnessed. It has also been observed that the experience of separation from the twin may be of the same order of upset as a separation from mother. However, while the awareness of separateness and the process of separation from mother is part of a developmental process, separation from a twin is not an automatic process. Where there is a lack of individual development in one or both twins this may lead to a crippling twinship that delays the individual maturation of each twin into adulthood. Separation from such an enmeshed twinship will be experienced as too terrifying to engage with. The sense of personal safety will reside within the twin relationship rather than internally in the individual twin.

Parental attitudes towards their twins will have an impact on the personality development of each of the twins. Twins are often treated as a unit by caregivers and others in their world. This makes it more difficult for them to work towards building a personal individuality, and to give up the exciting status of the twinship. The twin relationship engages many psychodynamic factors that will influence and create tensions in the interpersonal relations between the twins and their relationships with others, alongside environmental factors. These psychodynamic tensions will include the way each twin perceives and is perceived by the parents and other siblings, and the way each twin perceives the other twin and the relationship each of them has with mother and father. Among the many factors, the deep unconscious processes, including the phantasy twin of infancy, will influence the development of each twin in his relationships with all those around him, as already described.

The particular dynamic between the twins will also affect their individual development. A powerful twinning dynamic will be created by the factors of their lives: being born at roughly the same time, growing up together through similar parallel developmental stages, always having the other twin as a mirror, the projections from each twin into the other of the longed for ideal twin, parental attitudes, and the idealisation of the twinship. The feelings of rivalry, hostility or alternately closeness and strong dependency needs are common to all sibling relationships, but they are accentuated in twins. Numbers of studies have indicated that in some twin relationships, the bond between them is so close that establishing a separate existence for each twin is problematic. For some it seems that their world is shattered when they part, as if they have lost part of themselves. In these situations the twin relationship is a handicap rather than an advantage.

In some cases, the twin relationship creates a sexual intimacy that deepens the unconscious bonding between the twins—a subject often touched on in literature, perhaps exposing another fantasy about twins and the implied incestuous quality of their bond. We see this in mythology as well (see Chapter Five).

Several authors writing about sibling relationships have suggested that the need to find one's unique place in a world of similar others is the central psychic challenge we all face, and that we do this through the horizontal or lateral dimension of siblings, peers, partners, and many others throughout life (see Mitchell, 2003; Vivona, 2010). The dynamics of conflict and ambivalence in these lateral relationships exist in the same way as they do in the vertical relationships with parents, and their resolution will contribute a particular dimension to our psychic structure. This will involve a process of individual differentiation of self from other siblings, through conscious and unconscious actions. Differences between siblings will be amplified and similarities minimised. Rivalry will be lessened by creating difference while still maintaining an alliance with the other siblings for identification and support. Of course, for twins this development will be more complicated.

In twins, engaging in the processes of horizontal differentiation in order to establish a unique personal identity, to find ones pace in the world, will be muddied by the aspects of the twin relationship including the deep sensate bond between them and the idealisation of the twinning processes. The idealisation will occur both internally in each twin and between the twins, and in the perceptions of parents, other siblings and outsiders. As a result, twins may have to work harder to establish a rich personal identity. Where they do not sufficiently achieve this, this will affect all their relationships in both vertical (parents) and lateral (siblings, peers, marital partners, etc.) dimensions. The processes of differentiation and individuation will affect both the individual twins and their twin relationship so each twin will always have the other twin to take into account.

All children have to negotiate a realisation that one is not unique, there are other children, one is just one amongst others, the "crisis of non-uniqueness" (Mitchell, 2000), and to struggle for recognition of their unique self among similar others. How much more difficult this would be for twins, especially where they look and are treated as similar. Ideally, for siblings this non-uniqueness will be resolved as they find and accept their place in a social series, as equal but different.

This will be particularly potent for twins, especially for those that look so much alike and are presumed to be "two parts of one", sharing a personality by dividing the qualities between them, for instance, "the good one" and "the bad one", and so on. Add to these internal factors—the projection of the phantasy twin into the other twin so that the other twin is experienced as an extension of oneself, and we have so potent a cocktail against separateness and difference that the task of differentiation and individuation for twins is doubly hard.

Siblings exist not only in the outside world, but also in each child's inner world. They are mirrors of self that populate the child's inner social world. Twins Nancy and Janna Sipes (1998) describe having a twin being like a continuous dance in front of a mirror, "an unspoken closeness which transcends time, distance, and amount of physical contact" (p. 29). In their rather idealised account of twin relationships, they focus on the particular closeness twins may experience in the twin relationship, where twin bonding is pre-eminent amongst all their relationships, and the twin is a built-in soulmate. They consider the twin relationship is to be sacred territory that those outside it cannot understand or appreciate, and certainly not enter. They believe that being a twin is a gift, and their life-plan was to be together.

The child seeks his parents' recognition of his personal uniqueness amongst his siblings, and his worth amongst the other siblings, whether born or yet to be born, by his competition with the other siblings. If he can find recognition of his unique identity amongst others, he will develop a greater sense of his place in the world, with his hierarchy of positions. This would be one reason why twins seek so actively to establish whom is older. Particular problems may arise for twins at around the age of two, when they have what are felt to be urgent needs and cannot tolerate delay. Twins have to share their mother and take turns, at a time when this is not yet part of their understanding. As a result, they may resort more to biting to gain attention, temper tantrums, and other attention-seeking behaviour.

It is important to stress that relationships with siblings are not only rivalrous. They have many other dimensions that are crucial in enabling development in each one. They can be helpful, supportive, and enriching, and provide models for younger siblings to aspire to. Prophecy Coles (2014) emphasises the importance of sibling love and suggests that good sibling relationships have a profound effect on later loving and sexual relationships. Siblings are the models for later relationships. We have explored the view that the twin relationship is of a different order from other relationships and why this is so. Though the twinship may become a mature relationship, it is not so by nature. The heart of the twin relationship is narcissistic in character and considerable work is required for the twins to relinquish the safety of this rather stagnant place for the risky venture into the mature world of individual identity at the same time as valuing the twin relationship.

Where the entwined twinship is believed to be a dress rehearsal for all relationships, we have observed the way it can hinder the development of other relationships. Any partner will become a twin unless the twins shift out of twinning mode. There is not enough otherness in the twinship for it to serve as a developmental aid. As the Sipes write (1980), "As we grew up, our twinship did not. When we were together, no matter what our age, we would revert back to our childhood twin selves." Healthy development involves separation from the twin in a way that involves acceptance of the twin relationship as well as the development of each twin as an individual.

In summary

The nature of the twin relationship will be determined by many factors including hereditary factors and the way in which each twin of a particular genetic disposition negotiates the primary relationships with mother, father, the other twin, siblings, and others. Each twin has the complex dual task of forging a personal identity through individual psychic development, and also of negotiating the twin relationship. They will need to mature from the more narcissistic end of the twinship spectrum to one where both separateness and togetherness can be tolerated. In a twinship at the more narcissistic end of the spectrum, intense twinning processes will hamper the recognition and experience of the "otherness" of the other twin. Instead, the unity of the twinship will be idealised, in denial of the recognition of uniqueness of each individual twin. The idealisation of the twin relationship is based on essential internal loneliness that leads to a ubiquitous longing for a twin, a longing that emanates from the infant's earliest preverbal experiences with her mother.

While sharing many common elements with other sibling relationships, twin relationships differ in significant ways: the twins are always together—in utero, in mother's mind, and so on; twins share, to some extent, psychobiological rhythms; twins share an unconscious sensate bond that is a powerful force at the core of the twin relationship; and for twins, the unconscious phantasy twin created in the early relationship with mother may become concretised as the other twin becomes the embodiment of this phantasy twin, so compounding the intensity of the twinship.

All these factors create problems for twins in their development, but they may not necessarily be troubling in later life—this will depend on the degree of separateness and individuation and differentiation each of the twins is able to achieve. Where the twins cling to the psychic twinship for safety, and use it as a refuge or retreat, they are likely to be more inhibited in their individual development and their intimate relationships.

CHAPTER THREE

Twins apart

We have examined the importance of the establishment of separateness between twins, and the difficulties that an actual separation will pose for them. Whether through physical distance or death, the loss of a twin will create a situation in which the remaining twin has to negotiate particular processes to enable an emotional separation from their twin. It is the emotional separation that is the key to the resolution of the experience of loss of a twin, and that allows the remaining twin to be able to get on with life in a way that feels rewarding, and to be alive and real in a complex world.

Penelope Farmer (1996) noted after the death of her twin sister, "you need to separate; to confirm what it means to be an individual, single, by beginning at last to decipher the doubleness" (pp. 5–6). "For psychic and physical survival, let alone growth, probably, twins need to separate at some point, alive or dead." (ibid., p. 226)

Much has been written about twins together, their relationship, the dynamics between them, the antics they get up to, and the public fascination with them. There is also a considerable literature on the experience of the loss of a twin.

Most twin pregnancies result in the birth of one baby—the ratio is about one twin birth from every ten to twelve twin pregnancies.

Thus most twin pregnancies end with a single birth rather than with twins. Most of the twin loss occurs in the very early stages of the pregnancy and goes unnoticed by the mother. The losses for twin pregnancies are greater than for single foetuses (Boklage, 1995). MZ twins who share a placenta are particularly at risk, and the death of one of the twins in utero can result in an increased risk of cerebral impairment or neonatal death in the surviving twin.

Twins are at greater risk throughout the pregnancy and birth than are single babies, and they may face more challenges after birth as well. I will look at the loss of a twin at various different stages in development, both as a result of the death of one twin, but also at the sense of loss through separation, and the likely impact on the survivor or separated twin.

Separation and loss in twin relationships

Where both twin foetuses develop well and survive the birth, they will face separation from both mother and from their twin. Separation from the other twin may become a greater hurdle to face where one twin thrives in utero while the other suffers difficulties or even dies in the late stages of pregnancy. For all of us, issues of separation and loss will be central to the development of a sense of identity through infancy, childhood, and adulthood. We all face repeated losses that we have to negotiate. The experience of loss will be more marked in twins than it is in others because of the extra processes each twin has to manage in separating from the other twin. For twins, the establishment of separateness and separation may be experienced as a fundamental loss of the other twin.

The loss of a twin may generate a particular and sometimes unmanageable experience akin to feelings of annihilation, as has been well documented in literature and in accounts written by lone twins (see Woodward, 1998). Because of the nature of the twin relationship, the normal processes of mourning are more difficult to negotiate for a twin, especially when the narcissistic aspect of the twin relationship is a powerful part of the dynamic between the twins. In this situation, the loss of the twin may well be experienced as a profound loss of part of the self.

As Sigmund Freud (1917e) has described so eloquently in his work on mourning and melancholia, the feeling that a part of oneself has been lost in the bereavement is a central aspect of the process of mourning. Usually this feeling of being torn apart, or a diminution in the self, is gradually resolved as the mourner slowly relinquishes the lost person, and then regains the loved one in memory. The loss no longer feels like a gutting loss of part of the self, but becomes the loss of another person, vividly remembered.

The particular problem for twins lies in the existence of the deep, nonverbal sensate bond between them, one that provides a specifically intimate connection between them, and through which they feel closely identified with each other at a fundamental level. The loss of a twin would feel like an irrecoverable loss of part of the self. Unlike the ordinary processes of successful mourning for lost loved ones, the loss of a narcissistic object cannot be regained through the usual processes of relinquishment and then reinstatement in memory because the lost object is felt to be part of the self rather than another person. So the mourning twin may feel seriously depleted and unable to regain what has been lost. This is true for any narcissistic relationship, and given the close narcissistic aspects of identity of twins, is an inevitable difficulty in mourning where one twin is lost through separation or death.

Loss through separation

The difficulty some twins may have in leading separate lives is another aspect of the bound narcissistic relationship that twins share. Physical separation is not synonymous with emotional separation and individuation. It is evident from therapeutic work with twins how difficult it can be to achieve an adequate degree of emotional separation between the twins so that they can lead individually satisfying lives.

The idealisation of the twin relationship by the twins themselves and by others around them obscures the need for twins to redefine their relationship as they grow and develop in order to accommodate the changes that will inevitably occur in their lives. While the twin relationship diminishes in importance to allow individuality for each twin within it, there may be powerful feelings against such development, as it will be experienced as the twinship becoming of secondary importance. The central core of the twin relationship, the unconscious sensate aspects of it, will always remain for each twin, each with their own individual experience of it, in the same way that the earliest experiences of the baby with mother will endure.

It is possible for twins to move from the totality of the twinship into a mutual relationship that still values the twinship, but also allows each twin an opportunity to develop individually. This will require each twin to move away from and mourn the centrality of the twinship in their lives, and make space for both twin and individual relationships to co-exist. Often, one twin achieves this shift better than the other, and they will need to respect each other's achievements and vulnerabilities within these changes without being drawn back into a limiting twinship. An openness and willingness to communicate will be vital and the twins may need psychotherapeutic help to achieve this.

As I have already described, the twin infants have been together from the beginning and the twins interact with each other from early on in the pregnancy. During pregnancy, although they will not vie with each other for space until they have grown in size, they may be aware of the sounds and smell of each other from about sixteen weeks. There will be biorhythmic resonances between them though it is unclear when one twin foetus actually becomes conscious of the other twin. The pattern of relating between the twins that begins in utero persists after birth. The experience of the other twin and of mother both before and after birth would be laid down in the neural substrate all along the developmental line.

The late Charlotte Williams offered me a first-hand account of her difficulties in separating from her twin sister. She sent me a copy of an article she had published.

> The morning after my forty-fifth birthday, I woke up terrified, shaking in my bed with fear. I held on to my husband, both of us wondering what was going on. I couldn't bear the feeling of the sheets against my skin, so I got up, dressed, and began the day's routine, hoping that the terror would subside. It didn't. For the next few weeks I was so frightened I could barely sleep or eat; I was afraid to be alone, afraid to go outside, afraid even to listen to music. Everyday sights, such as trees waving in the wind, or twilight settling in, or looking at my name written down on a piece of paper, filled me with dread. Each time my husband and son went out, I wondered if I would ever see them again. I can remember watching them through the window of the house as they played football in the park opposite, feeling as though they might

disappear in a puff of smoke. Suddenly, it seemed that my entire world had collapsed around me, but I had no idea why.

Charlotte had made important changes to her life but she began to realise that, although these changes were significant, the major factor was her separation from her twin.

On our birthday, I hadn't been able to contact her, as she was on holiday. I'd expected her to phone, but she didn't. I knew why. Shortly before I moved, I'd visited her and we'd had an argument, during which she told me that she'd never loved me, or even liked me, that in fact she had no feelings for me at all. I was upset, but not that surprised. Ever since I'd met my husband, and moved out of the house I'd shared with her, our relationship had been under strain. I'd put her outburst down to jealousy that I was moving to my husband's hometown, away from her. I thought that, in time, she'd accept the situation; but I was wrong.

When I finally got hold of her, in a Spanish restaurant, I told her how terrible I was feeling. I'll never forget her reply. "Avocado and prawns," she said—she was ordering a starter. Then she added "Get some therapy!" and put the phone down.

Looking back, I don't blame her. In fact, I think she was right. It was sound advice, if brutally offered. I did get some therapy, and it helped. I realised that she had good reason to dislike me: ever since we were little, my father had always favoured me over her—a painful experience for any sibling, but especially so for a twin. As a result, in adult life, whenever I was happy, I felt it to be at my sister's expense, and was deeply guilty about it. Also, as children, our parents had been abroad, and we'd been sent to boarding schools at a young age. Because of that, I'd always looked to my sister to mother me, while she, for her part, had felt the need to control me.

At school, I usually got better marks than she did: when we took our eleven-plus, I passed, and she failed. As teenagers, I was confident, while she became shy and put on weight. We stuck together, but behaved like a single, split personality: she was the reliable, down-to-earth one, while I was the flighty, rebellious one. By the time we were adults, this distorted relationship had grown more and more tortuous, until finally, when we were well into our forties, she found the courage to break free.

Of course, you could put the problems between us down to the specific circumstances of our family history. But I don't think they were. Today, watching a close friend's twin boys grow up, I'm struck by how much they relate to each other, before anyone else comes into the picture. Sometimes it seems that the most significant person in their lives is not their mother, or their father, but the mirror image of themselves they see before them every hour of every day as they grow up—their twin. So no wonder that when my mirror image finally disappeared, it felt like a bereavement, or worse, as though my self had got lost somewhere, and no longer existed in the real world.

Charlotte commented that she once described the relationship as "a marriage you've been in all your life, only you don't know you're in it".

Loss through death

"The surviving twin will never have known life without a (mostly constant) partner of the same age and may find the loss deeply disturbing." (Bryan, 1999, p. 186)

The perinatal period is particularly crucial for twins. Death or disability is much more common in multiple births than for single children. Parents faced with the death of one twin at or near birth will have to manage not only their own loss, but also that of the surviving twin. Parental reactions to the surviving baby are likely to be mixed. The joy at having a live baby will be marred by the death of the other.

This considerable loss to the parents, and to the surviving twin, whatever the age of the twins or nature of the twin relationship, will create particularly difficult developmental tasks for the surviving twin. For the parents, their loss will be complicated—while grieving for one baby, they also have a live baby to celebrate and attend to and there may be painful confusion between the live baby and the dead one. The joy is laden with mourning and loss. The live baby will be a constant reminder of the dead one. As a result the live twin may well suffer profound psychic injuries that are not immediately apparent. The parents will need to pay particular attention and offer reassurance to the surviving twin at the same time as grieving for the loss of one of their children.

Although death at birth or in the womb are natural events, they seem contradictory and against the natural order of life. The fusion of birth and death results in hurt and bitter disappointment for the parents, but may also create confusion and a sense of unreality. While this complexity is especially acute when a twin dies during pregnancy or soon after birth, it will occur at the death of one twin at any age.

Feelings may become polarised for the parents. The surviving baby may seem to be more precious to them, and they may become fearful that he too will die. They may start to be over-protective in compensation, creating insecurity in the surviving baby. Should the parents' grief become overwhelming, the surviving twin may feel devalued, as if the dead baby has primary importance and he has no proper place in their lives. The surviving twin may lose confidence in himself and in his potential to grow and develop.

An opposite response that parents may exhibit is the rejection of the surviving twin where they feel unable to tolerate their feelings of helplessness in the face of their severe loss. The dead twin may be idealised and comparisons with the live twin would be unfavourable to the survivor. Idealisation of the dead baby would make it more difficult for them to accept the survivor fully. The fact that the dead twin will never become a difficult, demanding baby and will only be remembered as perfect and godlike, rather echoes the Castor–Pollux myth (Chapter Five).

Even where the surviving twin is welcomed, the parents will also be preoccupied with the dead baby and their loss. Their attention is divided by contradictory feelings. The painful emptiness created by the loss of one baby contrasts with the mother's increasing emotional commitment to the live baby. The missing twin will always be present in the reflection of the surviving twin.

This was beautifully expressed by Elizabeth Pector (2006, p. 27) in a poem she wrote after one of her twin children died:

Footprints

Tiny feet
That should be taking baby steps
Instead left
Giant Footprints
Embedded in my heart.

Matching Feet
Now walking, take their baby steps
Alone

They should have walked together
But only one will blaze a trail
His trailhead marked by
Giant Footprints
Left there by his stillborn twin:
Buried wombmate memories that linger deep within.

Although a twin relationship creates additional developmental obstacles for each twin, the death of the one twin would not have freed the surviving twin from all the difficulties of individual development within a twinship. It may instead have added an additional developmental burden, in that the image of the dead twin may hold and represent in the mind of the surviving twin the powerful projections linked with life and death, survival and revenge. As the dead twin is no longer available to test these phantasies against reality, the surviving twin may be left with unmanageable feelings about the death of the twin, especially those associated with a fear that the survivor caused the death of the other twin—a common idea when one twin dies perinatally.

Where one of the twins dies at or around birth, the surviving newborn baby will experience not just separation from, but also the absence of, the other twin, and a mother who in her grieving may not be as attentive to her new baby as she would like to be. For the live twin, guilt at surviving and a confusion of identity with the dead twin may affect the personality development of the infant.

Even though one twin has died, it is important that the twinship be remembered and respected, and that the surviving twin is given information and support in relation to the loss of the other twin. The more open the parents are about the loss for the surviving twin, the better are the chances that the survivor will be able to manage the loss of the twin without undue trauma or feelings of guilt. The earlier this support is offered, the better, as even a young child will have his own sensate and perhaps later memories of the lost twin and will need help understanding and dealing with the loss.

It helps the parents with their grieving if they are able to distinguish mentally between the two babies, so that the sense of confusion between the babies and the life/death situation can diminish. Seeing and holding the dead baby enables the parents to see it as a person in its own right. They will better be able to mourn their loss. Naming the dead baby and having a burial or funeral to mark the existence of the dead baby also helps the grieving process. It may also be important to the parents that with the death of one of their twins, they lose their status as parents of twins.

We all have heard stories about our birth, or if we have not we long to know. The stories that are woven around the birth of all babies are also very important to the surviving twin's sense of acceptance or rejection by the parents, and to the infant's tolerance of feelings of guilt and anxiety in relation to the death of the twin. These stories are a combination of fact and phantasy based on the emotional experiences at the time and later in life. I call them "birth myths" because they are stories linked with our unconscious sense of our identities and ourselves. The surviving baby has not yet developed the capacity to deal with the traumatic event of the death of her twin and her experience of her grieving parents. The triumph of her survival and the death of her twin will create a conflict for her, and the surviving baby will need help dealing with this so that she can eventually mourn her loss in more than a very rudimentary way.

The parents' reaction to the birth is very important to the surviving twin's sense of acceptance or rejection by the parents, and to the infant's tolerance of feelings of guilt and anxiety in relation to the death of her twin. If this is not available she may be left with a profound sense of an unmanageable experience. The infant is greatly dependent on the parents to help her emerge from this complex situation without feeling extremely tormented, perhaps suffering feelings of fragmentation. But the parents have such conflicting feelings themselves at this time, that the situation is inherently fraught with difficulty.

Examples of such difficulties are common and often based on lack of knowledge or misunderstanding. Some surviving twins feel responsible for the death of their twin, feeling they "took too much", when parents have indicated that the dead twin lacked nourishment, for whatever reason, such as an inadequate placenta. The survivor may believe she was too greedy, took all the nourishment and as a result the other twin starved. I have heard of surviving twins feeling they are greedy monsters, murderers. Mothers, too, in this situation will feel guilty that they were not able to provide adequate nourishment to both babies. Some surviving twins believe they had kicked the twin in utero causing fatal damage. A surviving female twin may feel she can never match up to the lost idealised, preferred dead twin brother.

Often each twin is referred to as "the twin", whether or not they have both survived, and surviving twins may well resent being regarded as a singleton, as Case (1993) has illustrated in her book about twins who have lost the co-twin. The enduring twinship exists not only in the minds of twins themselves, but also in the perception of others, most notably their parents. Parents have also described feeling upset and angry if the surviving twin is referred to as a singleton after the death of one twin (Swanson, 2001). In response to the question, "When is a twin not a twin?" Swanson states categorically, "NEVER". Thus it is important for the surviving twin's development of a sense of self that both the birth stories and the parental attitude in talking to the surviving child reflect the fact that the other twin has died and that it is not the fault of the survivor.

Some surviving twins create and maintain an imaginary twin to replace the lost twin (and to represent the unconscious phantasy twin of early infancy). As already discussed in Chapter One, other conscious childhood imaginary twins tend to disappear, but the conscious and unconscious phantasy of the dead twin would remain a potent relationship for the surviving twin. This imaginary twin may be used as a refuge from developmental moves that provoke too much anxiety, or to protect the surviving twin from her painful experience of loss and the perhaps unmanageable anxiety about the loss. However, an imaginary twin is not always a hindrance to development. It may also be employed as an aid to mourning and further development by helping the surviving twin regulate the current extreme anxieties until they become more manageable. These imaginary twins are often felt to be, and are spoken to as if they are, actually present.

Twins who lose the other twin later in life will have conscious memories of the other twin as well as the deep unconscious connections and somatic memories of the lost twin. The profoundly painful experience of losing a twin may leave the survivor feeling the loss as a threat to their belief in their own survival. This may be experienced as the psychic death of the self as a twin. These very primitive feelings may be experienced as a sense of annihilation of the self. The protection of a live twin relationship has been lost and this loss may be felt as the death of part of the self, or as if part of the body had been hacked off. The surviving twin may wish to grow another half to replace the lost twin or may respond by taking on the characteristics of the dead twin as if to reinstate the lost twin. For some, the internalised dead twin may be active in the mind of the survivor, seeking revenge—a very threatening internal situation. If this state of mind remains untempered, the experience of the death of the twin may precipitate an emotional breakdown at a later time.

The loss of any sibling is traumatic and is difficult to process. The loss of a twin would be even more so, because of the earliest sensate resonances between the twins. Joan Woodward (1998) lost her twin when she was three and a half years old. She writes that she experienced a loss of known boundaries, and a sense of loss of identity. Some lone twins deny the death of the twin and believe in a fantasied idealised reunion with the lost twin. They take refuge in the internal idealised twinship as a defence against mourning the loss of the other twin. The denial of loss may lead the surviving twin to keep the dead twin alive by living for both. Alternately the survivor may feel that he has died along with his co-twin and live a restricted half-life. It is as if the surviving twin has a foot in both camps, life and death, where death is a friend, a close companion, personified by lost twin. This will lead the surviving twin to a situation where he feels as if he is only half a person.

Woodward (1998), in her book *The Lone Twin*, sought to understand the connection between the experience of a deep loss and its effect on the formation of a sense of self or identity. In her view the loss of a twin is a profound experience for most surviving twins and will have a marked, or even severe, effect on their lives, particularly for same-sex twins. This would be particularly marked where the death of the twin had occurred in a traumatic way.

Twins who have lost the other twin before the age of six months will suffer the most marked or severe effects of twin loss. Woodward attributes this to two factors. First, the loss has happened at an age when the surviving twin is pre-verbal and cannot speak about the loss or grieve properly. The capacity to symbolise is still developing and therefore the capacity to understand the loss is limited. The surviving twin will be overwhelmed with feelings that she cannot yet manage.

Second, the surviving twin is caught up in her parents' feelings about losing a baby as well as her own, and as we have explored, the parents' feelings will be very mixed. It may also be that the surviving twin loses trust in the parents who were unable to prevent the death of the other twin, and may fear for her own life.

What is clear is that the loss of a twin will have long-standing effects on the survivor. Helen Macdonald, in her autobiographical book, *H is for Hawk*, links her obsession with creating jesses for her new hawk with her experience as a newborn of being in an incubator with tubes in and out of her. Her twin brother had died at birth, and she felt she was the lucky one. No one ever spoke about the tragedy. Years later, when she did find out, she felt the news was surprising—but not so surprising. She had always felt part of her was missing, "an old, simple absence". She questions whether her obsession with birds was connected with that first loss, with something she did not know she had lost, but knew it had gone.

The book is a study of mourning, for her dead twin and her father. It is an account of twinning attachments, to her father and her goshawk. It is as if her goshawk, Mabel, was her embodied soul, as in Philip Pullman's daemons (see Chapter Six). She raises questions about her identity, an identity she felt she was losing in relation to father's death, and to the arduous process of training her hawk. She felt that she was lacking, not good enough, bad, and so on, rather than that the difficulty lay with the hawk.

Twins have never known what it is not to be a twin. They are never "un-twinned", in the same way that after the death of a parent, we do not cease to be the child of that parent. After the loss of a twin, the twin relationship lives on in memory and the deep unconscious aspects of the psyche, and the twin relationship may be acted out in ways that are destructive to their other relationships.

One of the many books I came across about the effects of the death of a twin is that by Case (1993). She quotes from a number of letters about the feelings generated by the death of a twin. I have selected some as they indicate particular aspects of the twinship and its enduring nature. The enmeshed nature of a narcissistic twinship is evident in the following:

> Karrie writes, "A major part of my life and of me was laid to rest when Kathy died. For 23 years one-half of me was her, and I think

it always will be. Just as a part of me is gone, a part of Kathy lives on through me." (p. 18)

So, even when one twin has died, the survivor feels that the twins have not separated, indeed are not separable. Together they will always form a unit, a lifelong twinship. Like Castor and Pollux, the twins will remain forever united.

Where the death of the twin feels intolerable and unbelievable, some twins may seek to maintain the twinship through spiritual union with the dead twin, in denial of loss. One year after the death of her twin, Caroline describes a Narcissus-like dream in which she sees her dead twin in the flowing river. She writes:

> Since Mary's death my whole world has become clouded. I have become overwhelmed with fears of isolation and abandonment. In a sense, I search for her. I surround myself with pictures, talk about her constantly, relive memories, and share every thought and prayer with her. Despite my efforts to survive, I feel that it is not natural to be physically separated from her. In fact is seems terribly wrong. I keep thinking, "I am going to die because Mary and I must always be together". I feel a separation from Mary that causes physical pains in my chest. On the other hand, I have never felt closer to her, as we are now joined by a spiritual bond which is unique to us. (ibid., p. 50)

It is still early days in the mourning process for Caroline. She lives a half-life, with a foot in both camps, life and death. She has idealised the twinship and elevated it to spiritual and mystical plains. Unless she can relinquish her narcissistic attachment to her idealised dead twin, and acknowledge and mourn her death, she will remain in the realm of unresolved grief.

Sarah's twin died in utero, four months into the pregnancy. I suspect that her experience of the loss of her twin is based mainly on her "birth story" and the attitude of her parents. Nevertheless, she suffers intense survivor guilt, and a sense of having to live for her lost twin as well as herself. Aged twenty-two, she writes:

> One moment, I can feel devastatingly lonely and not be able to wait for the day when I can die to go meet him in heaven. Just to hug

him and tell him how much I love him. Yet at the same time I feel so
incredibly guilty for being alive, like I don't deserve it. (ibid., p. 63)

Like Caroline above, Sarah has idealised the lost twinship. She has created an imaginary twin to replace her lost twin brother and to try to
cope with her feelings of guilt and loneliness.

The denial of the loss of the twin will be at great cost to personal
identity. Sometimes it takes many years before the surviving twin can
begin to mourn the loss. Where the survivor is able to mourn the dead
twin, this is likely to enrich the life of the surviving twin and allow the
growth of individuality and maturity. Thus Sandy writes:

Seventeen years have passed. As long without Karen as with her.
I now realise that I've been running instead of dealing with the pain
of the loss. I stopped denying the loss and I'm able to be aware of
my body, opinions and thoughts. I'm now developing a life that
includes Karen as a fond memory. I'm not forsaking Karen, instead
I'm honoring myself and the life I have to live. (ibid., p. 28)

This further development can be experienced as finding a new freedom.
Paula discovers the value of separateness after the death of her twin.

And now? Finding oneself. Knowing one's capabilities. Finding
sudden joy in knowing that I could attempt something: an assign-
ment at work, writing poems, accomplishing a new weight-loss
program, all without the twin-oriented dependence. Laughter coming easily (it never did before). A new person discovering capabilities and potential never known before. (ibid., p. 42)

Both these accounts show that it is possible to achieve separation from
a twin after the death of one, and therefore to mourn the death of the
twin. There will no doubt still be an important residue of the twinship, a
deep conscious and unconscious bond with the dead twin, but it is possible to have a separate and continuing life after a twin has died.

Woodward (1998) considers that the most marked effect on the life of
the surviving twin occurs in same-sex twins, whether MZ or DZ. Whatever the sex of the twins or their zygosity I think that the major factor
would be the nature of the twin relationship, the degree of identification between them and the extent to which they would have established

an individual identity. The narcissistic core of the twinship will make grieving for a twin a more difficult task and the loss would feel more profound than the loss of other siblings.

After the death of a twin the surviving twin will often try to find a new twinship within intimate relationships such as marriage or even with their children, as if the twin way of relating is so central to her way of being it is hard for her to be any other way.

Both unconscious and conscious aspects of the twin relating will be encountered in lone twins, regardless of the age at which their twin dies. As we have seen above, the capacity of the survivor to separate from the dead twin and mourn the loss varies according to the nature of the twin relationship. Unconscious factors relating to the twinship play a major part in the success or otherwise of mourning, and are an enduring factor in the surviving twin's ability to establish a life without the lost twin. The lost twin always casts a shadow on the survivor, even if the death was before birth in the later stages of the pregnancy or in the first few months of life, before any conscious memory of the event is possible. To what extent this is a function of unconscious memory traces or parental input and attitudes is difficult to discern.

Much is written about the "vanishing twin" syndrome, and there are many accounts of people discovering that they were part of a twin pregnancy and that the other twin died in the early stages of the pregnancy, in utero. There are stories of such twin survivors suffering extreme loneliness and feeling an unresolved longing, until they discover that they had originally had a twin who did not survive the pregnancy. Although the senses develop very early in the foetus, it is most unlikely that the twin lost in the early stages of pregnancy will have had much impact on the live twin. For most twins, there will have been two amniotic sacs and two placentas, and they will have had no contact with each other in the early stages, when most losses occur. It is only in the last few months of the pregnancy that greater contact and impact will occur. This would most likely enter the sensate awareness of the twins creating somatic memories and would affect their emotional development.

It is most likely that the profound sense of longing and loneliness suffered by some people who had been part of a twin pair but where the other foetus vanished early on, is attributable to the longing we all feel based on our very early experiences with mother, the deep unconscious understanding we experienced with her. We all long for a perfect understanding with another, a soulmate, a twin, and discovering that one had a vanished twin in utero will play into this.

Two written accounts of the experience of the loss of a twin have struck me as highly illustrative of the difficult processes of mourning in twins.

Saul Diskin (2001) describes his experience of his very close relationship with his twin brother, Marty, their separation as adults and, after prolonged treatment, Marty's death.

The intense and visceral entanglement of the twin boys when aged five is evident when Marty climbs up onto the roof and Saul, witnessing him at the edge of the parapet wall, believes Marty will try to fly off. He was so sick with fear that he vomited and his visceral reaction to the imagined loss of his twin was so severe he had to be hospitalised. As he says, fifty years later, he didn't have to try to remember what he felt when he thought his twin was dying—his stomach told him. This visceral connection between twins who grew up doing everything together persisted throughout their lives.

Diskin believes no sibling is ever as close as twins. They suffer from a lack of uniqueness and confusion of identities. He felt he could not tell where one of them ended and the other began. They would taunt each other with death by taking risks, leaving him wondering, if Marty died, would they both die? There was also a murderous rivalry between them, which they sometimes used to try to find a degree of separateness from each other.

The twin bond was binding, yet they felt the need to find a separate identity. "Stronger than reason, a feeling, a tropism, both informed and drove our young minds and bodies to cast off the comfortable protection of twinhood and seek something unknowable and frightening to us—separation." (Diskin, 2001, p. 25) When they had achieved this, "what remained was the shadow of the ache of our loss" (p. 38), with a continuing power to strongly affect each other.

Many years later Marty developed leukaemia, leading Saul to wonder, "if he dies is it the end of me?" It was agreed that Saul would donate bone marrow to Marty to help him survive. Saul wrote to Marty, "if you died first I would have all those years to live without you, but if I died first it would be the end of the twins because without the transplant you would soon follow" (ibid., p. 106). This indicates not only the close connection through the treatment, but also the deep unconscious experience of their twinship, the deep essence of the relationship, and the extreme pain and anxiety at the prospect of the loss of the twinship.

He writes of the "unbearable pain of being without you. It is the feeling of having some integral part of me physically torn out of me, something living in me, but not entirely mine. I would survive your death as you would survive mine. But something … would be finished for me, would be stilled forever." (ibid., p. 214) He felt there was a part of both of them that never fully separated from each other, as if there was no entirely discrete other.

After Marty died, he felt, "The twins were gone. I was alone." (ibid., p. 120) He was clear that dead is dead and no connection would exist between them after Marty's death, but "He'll live for me within the ache of memory. But what will I be … without the other part? Will the emptiness ever be filled?" (ibid., p. 272) However, he also described how mourning the death of his twin eventually allowed him to fall in love.

Another moving account is that of Timothy Knatchbull, talking on BBC Radio 4 and in his book, *From a Clear Blue Sky* (2010). He described the hour-by-hour sharing with his twin brother, seeing his brother as a mirror. When his brother died tragically, he experienced an "internal psychic loss", was left feeling utterly lost, profoundly disorientated, with a deep sadness and loneliness, as if he had "lost part of self", that is, he was both a mourner and victim. Knatchbull describes how he lost inner peace when his twin brother was killed suddenly and violently.

The twins, Nicholas Timothy and Timothy Nicholas, were different sizes at birth. They shared a room and dressed alike. Their "identical appearance confused everyone including us" (Knatchbull, 2010, p. 9). They "shared genes, names, clothes, habits and hobbies, but not toys". And, he adds crucially, they were very different characters. He believed that the twinship created fun, constant companionship, and total empathy with each other. The twinship was central to their lives and in some ways he feels they were married to each other (as did Charlotte Williams)—it was a relationship for life. He believes their intellectual abilities were heightened by twinship as they tapped into each other's knowledge and processing power.

When his twin was killed violently by the bomb planted by the IRA to kill their grandfather, Lord Mountbatten, Tim Knatchbull was badly injured, but survived. He did not know how to live his life without Nick. "There was an underlying flaw to the story of Nick's death because it went against the basic truth of our twinhood: physically Nick was more robust than me so if one of us were going to die it would be me, not him." (ibid., p. 125) But he also had a flash of relief at being alive.

He was in disbelief that his twin had died. He felt numb, complicated by the experience of death of his twin/self, of a shared identity not yet fully differentiated. He felt Nick was just absent and that he was still sharing life with him. He recalled a conversation with Norris McWhirter whose MZ twin Ross was shot by the IRA. Norris told him it felt like an amputation, not a death.

Knatchbull felt he needed to be as intimate with Nick's body in death as he had in life. He had not seen Nick's actual body and felt he needed to examine the forensic photos of Nick after death. He felt this led him to feel more balanced and able to begin to mourn. He returned to the house alone to say a final goodbye to Nick, knowing he was dead. He states, "I'd choose to come back again as a twin, if I could have you again." (ibid., p. 373) His book details his shift from an idyllic (idealised) childhood twinship through mourning into adolescence and adult separateness.

Penelope Farmer compiled a comprehensive insightful anthology on twins, spurred on by her own experience of being a twin, and having to cope with her feelings of loss after her twin sister died. She created the book to keep in contact with the lost twinship and her profound loss.

She describes their separation at age seventeen, when she experienced feelings of loss for the first time in relation to her twin, but without being able to understand the feelings. She felt utter gloom and desolation and only years later, on reflection, did she realise what her feelings were about: "the loss I felt was more than anything that of twinness; bringing the realisation for the first time, perhaps, that like everyone else, I was alone, finally, and liable to remain that way. I did not know it in my head but wept for it in my body ..." (Farmer, 1996, p. 227)

When her twin was dying of cancer thirty-eight years later, she experienced viscerally the growing awareness of the deep loss her twin's death would mean for her: "all this time I had this profound feeling that it was, yet wasn't, my flesh that was dying" (ibid., p. 227–228). But she was able to separate herself from her twin rather than, as some lone twins report, feeling forever that they too have died. "But as I began to emerge into the relief of understanding that I was not her, that I was still very much alive, along with gratitude and guilt, came a guilty yet deep exhilaration. I felt in a terrible, wonderful way as if I was, literally, feeding, being given life by her dead flesh. (ibid., p. 228)

She recounts how much of the material she found on twins trying to cope with the death of one of them, reflected the deeply physical way in which she too had experienced the absence of her twin, her illness, and finally her death.

In Chapter Five, I will look at various practices in relation to the death of one or both twins in various societies.

In summary, it is important to acknowledge that the loss of a twin at whatever age will have a profound effect on the surviving twin. The intense internal sensate bond between the twins makes mourning a more difficult and complex task for twins than it is for others.

CHAPTER FOUR

Twins in society

The media rarely miss an opportunity to create excitement about politicians, performers, and celebrities who are twins. There appears to be a divide between those who happen to be a twin and where the twinship is not relevant to the area of their importance or talent as famous people but is nevertheless hyped by the media, and those twins who use the twin relationship as part of their celebrity status or their performance. Given the unreliability of the media, it is often difficult to work out whether it is the famous twins who have used their twinship as part of their celebrity, or whether the media, searching for a new exciting angle, have picked up on the twinship because it supposedly magnifies some aspect of the celebrity. At the heart of this attention is our fascination with twins and what the twin relationship represents in our imaginative lives.

An internet search of "famous twins" or "celebrity twins" will offer lists of twins in the limelight under titles like "Seven Most Famous Twins of all Time", or "Famous Twins—Top Ten List". So we get an indiscriminate variety of twinships listed, like Jenna and Barbara Bush, Mary Kate and Ashley Olsen, Reggie and Ronnie Kray, Ronde and Tiki Barber, Abigail van Buren and Anne Landers, Robin and Maurice Gibb, Tegan and Sara Quin, Romulus and Remus, Elvis Presley, Jaroslaw and

Lech Kacynski, Chang and Eng Bunker, Justin Timberlake, and Patty and Selma Bouvier. Never heard of some of them? Me neither!

What is of interest in terms of this book is first the excitement about finding that some celebrities are twins or have had a twin who has died, or have twin children; and second, those famous twins who have used the twin relationship as a major factor of their celebrity. In both these situations, the idealisation of the twin relationship plays a key part in our perception of the twin status of the celebrity/celebrities. But in some cases it may also indicate something about the close intertwining of the twins in their specific relationship.

An exploration of the relationships of some of the "famous" twins will help us understand more about twin relationships in general, as well as our perceptions of these particular twins, and the way the celebrity twins view, use, or ignore their own twin relationship. There are many more examples than I can possibly examine, so I have chosen those that seemed to me to express something particular about the twin relationship and the uses of it.

Sporting twins

Mo Farah, Olympic, World, and European champion runner, has a twin brother Hassan who is also athletic, but was left in Somalia when Mo came to the UK with his family. Apparently Hassan was ill and could not travel. When their father returned to Somalia to fetch Hassan, he could not find him as the family he was staying with had moved. So Mo and Hassan were parted for twelve years. Mo felt he had lost his twin brother and best friend. They both talk of the heartbreak of the separation, and the joy of the reunion. Mo writes in his autobiography that part of him had been missing all the time they were separated, that they are not different people but, instead, part of the same person. Mo feels that Hassan's absence had created a void that was filled when they were reunited.

Hassan too feels they were torn apart by the separation. He and Mo apparently had such a close bond that they slept in the same bed and shared food from the same plate. They were inseparable. When Mo departed he felt he was left with an empty space in his heart, that he had lost the other half of himself. They both felt they had a special connection in which each would instinctively feel what the other person was going through—even if they were thousands of miles apart.

We can see from their comments about their separation the degree to which each of these twins has invested in the narcissistic aspects of the twin relationship. Although they were living very separate lives, they both felt an essential part of them was missing. This is also reflected in their other relationships. Hassan married a woman who is a twin. Mo feels that twins are "in their blood". Mo's wife, Tania, gave birth to twin girls. They seem to need to find parallel lives (so common in enmeshed twin pairs), and Hassan says that he and his wife keep trying to have a set of twins, to be the same as Mo and his wife. The quest for sameness and equality is a common feature in twins who feel deeply entwined with each other.

Despite considering themselves to be two parts of the same person, there are clear differences between Mo and Hassan. Obviously Hassan did not have the wonderful advantages that Mo did in his training as an athlete, his schooling, or his life, and Hassan has not achieved the athletic status that Mo has. We don't know how well he might have done had he had equivalent advantages. But it is interesting to find that Mo apparently could not read or write as he suffers from dyslexia. Hassan, on the other hand, has a natural talent for learning, a sharp mind, and works as an IT consultant. So there are ways in which Mo and Hassan are very different but perhaps view these complementary traits as a way of managing the whole.

It is also indicative of the depth of the twin relationship that, while living in London, Mo found in a cousin with whom he stayed, a substitute twin. He did not want to be separated from his cousin when his parents split up. He felt his cousin Mahad was the closest thing he had to his twin, Hassan. Mo and Mahad did everything together. When Mo's parents separated, Mo chose to stay in London with Mahad, as he did not want to go through the trauma again of being separated from someone with whom he had so closely bonded. It is common for twins to create a twin bond with significant other people in their lives. It is frequently a spouse who becomes the new twin, but in Mo's case it was his cousin. I do not know whether this has been a feature in his relationship with his wife.

Sir Henry Cooper was a champion boxer who had a twin brother, George. Henry was the elder twin by twenty minutes. They were born on 3 May 1934 in Westminster. Both boys inherited their father's love of boxing and first discovered their prowess in the school playground, where they invariably stood up for one another. They were considered "right little ruffians".

According to an obituary in the *Telegraph* after his twin brother George died, Henry wrote in his autobiography in 1972 that he and George were always very close. The only time they parted was when he got married. Even then, George came to live with Henry until he married, as their father had retired and had gone to live in Margate with their mother.

> We went to school together, we went boxing together, we were together in the Army. We look alike, we think alike, in temperament we're similar and often we catch ourselves repeating each other's remarks. Throughout our boxing lives I would go on first so that I wouldn't be worrying over George's fight when I got into the ring.

Henry won the ABA light-heavyweight crown at eighteen and subsequently competed for Britain at the 1952 Helsinki Olympics. Although George had a heavier punch than his brother, he suffered badly from cut eyes and at the age of sixteen survived rheumatic fever, which sidelined him for a year. Prior to turning professional he suffered a broken thumb and—according to Henry—never punched so hard again.

The Cooper twins turned professional and became celebrities. Henry went on to become one of the most successful British boxers of all time, fighting and beating Muhammad Ali in 1963. George remained prone to cuts, eventually retiring in November 1964. He became his brother's trainer and confidant.

The closeness in this twinship is evident, and there is a sense that each brother, looking at the other twin, sees himself. So they work together, watch out for each other and remain united in their professional life as they did in their personal lives.

Criminal twins

Reginald and **Ronald Kray** were notorious gangsters, deeply involved in organised crime in the East End of London during the 1950s and 1960s. With their gang, The Firm, they were involved in armed robberies, arson, protection rackets, assaults, and murders. They also owned nightclubs in the West End where they mixed with and entertained

well-known entertainers, politicians, and the rich and famous including Frank Sinatra, Diana Dors, Judy Garland, Labour MP Tom Driberg,
Lord Boothby, Lucien Freud, and Francis Bacon. They owned, for a
while, Esmeralda's Barn in Mayfair, bought from the notorious Peter
Rachman, and were involved in the prostitution of young boys.

A ruthless pair, they were commonly known as the Kray Twins. The
twin relationship was central to them and they were encouraged in
their criminal lives both by their rivalry as boxers in their early lives,
and by their apparent invincibility as a formidable twin pair. They were
fearless and uncontained in their violence, directing it at whomever
dared to cross them, whether it was in the army when they enrolled for
a very brief time, in prison awaiting a court martial for absence from
the army without leave, or in prison cells after their dishonourable
discharge from the army for bad behaviour.

The Kray twins' criminal records ended their boxing careers, and they
gradually moved into protection rackets, arson, hijacking, and armed
robbery. They associated with other violent criminals (the Richardson
gang), landlords (the infamous and corrupt Rachman) and a banker
(Alan Cooper, who was seeking protection by them from the Richardson
gang). They used their power to rule and corrupt. In 1960 Ronnie Kray
was imprisoned for 18 months for running protection rackets.

As John Pearson wrote in the *Independent* in 1997, after new evidence
emerged since writing his book about the Krays, published in 1972:

> Ronald, a homosexual, was seriously psychotic, and his identical
> twin brother, Reginald, was living on his nerves—and Gordon's gin.
> Both were palpably dangerous. But despite, or possibly because of
> this, the twins were extraordinarily successful in their chosen line
> of business. In their dark blue suits and chauffeur-driven cars they
> were essentially early figures of the enterprise culture, criminal
> entrepreneurs who made large amounts of tax-free money from a
> vast and efficiently administered protection racket, mostly oper-
> ated with other criminals.
>
> They were the enforcers of the underworld, "Percentage Men",
> whose reputation was so fearsome that hardened criminals obeyed
> them. Much of the Krays' money came from the arsonists, gam-
> blers and fraudsters they saved from trouble. They had connections
> with the American Mafia, "protecting" their gambling interests in
> London together with the sale of stolen bearer bonds in Europe.

Many West End clubs paid them to keep out of trouble, and the Krays had a knack of getting money out of any crime they heard of either by threats or extortion. They could be useful if expensive allies—and lethal enemies.

The Kray twins were clearly not without charm, and became part of the swinging London scene in the 1960s. The 1960s were good years for the Kray twins, and Ronnie felt they were the best years of their lives, with the Beatles and the Rolling Stones ruling pop music, Carnaby Street ruling the fashion world, and the Kray twins (in his eyes) ruling London. They felt they were untouchable and behaved as if they were. Their sense of being special, as twins emboldened by their dual bulk, led them to believe in their superiority and invulnerability.

Eventually, an intrepid Detective Superintendent, Leonard "Nipper" Read of Scotland Yard, managed to gather enough evidence despite the East End "wall of silence", the high-level political corruption that offered protection to the Kray brothers, and the general terror of being a witness against these monsters. They were arrested in 1968 along with other members of their "firm". They were tried and both sentenced to life imprisonment for at least thirty years before parole could be considered. During their separate long-term imprisonments, they continued to run a bodyguard and protection service with the connivance of their elder brother Charlie and another accomplice.

Both were considered to be mentally unstable since their early days. Ronnie was certified insane (probably paranoid schizophrenia) and removed to Broadmoor Hospital where he lived for the rest of his life until he died in 1995 of a heart attack, aged 61. Reggie was a category A prisoner, denied all liberties, and was not allowed to mix with other prisoners. His prisoner status was later downgraded and he was moved to a less secure prison. He became a born-again Christian and was finally released from prison in 2000 at the age of 66 on compassionate grounds, as he was found to have inoperable cancer of the bladder. He died shortly after his release and was buried alongside his brother Ronnie.

A story about Reggie's marriage to Frances Shea in 1965 demonstrated the depth of their connection with each other as twins, and their sense of the exclusiveness of their relationship. Frances died in 1967, apparently by suicide. But an ex-lover and fellow inmate of Reggie's at Maidstone prison alleged that two days after her death Ronnie had confessed to Reggie that he had murdered Frances, as he was jealous of her relationship with "his Reggie".

These "professionals of violence" illustrate not only their use of violence to gain and maintain power and money, but crucially they show us the damaging consequences of their being twins enmeshed in a twinship that they used for perverse means, a twinship that crippled them both as individuals.

Political twins

Mark and **Carol Thatcher** are an example of twins between whom rivalry has flourished at the expense of any more rewarding aspects of the twin relationship, perhaps exacerbated by favouritism. They are the twin children of the late Prime Minister, Lady Margaret Thatcher, and unusually for twins are known and quoted largely for their differences, and for being the children of a woman of immense power, financial resources, and status. Their relationship is distant, disapproving, and competitive in indirect ways. They apparently dislike each other and have very little contact, especially since the death of their mother.

Mark displays the arrogance and triumphalism of a favoured twin. He failed to achieve good grades at school, and failed his accountancy exams. But he seems to have been favoured by his mother. He was the blond golden boy who despite his many misdemeanours, was repeatedly bailed out by his mother. When he became lost in the Sahara during the 1982 Paris-Dakar rally, Mrs Thatcher's intervention led to a large-scale search involving six military aircraft. Mark arrogantly had boasted that he had done nothing to prepare for the rally.

Mark was regarded as his mother's favourite child. He inherited his father's title and baronetcy. He amassed a great deal of money, and he was involved in a number of lucrative deals in the Middle East amid claims that he was using his mother's influence to promote and secure them. Several of Mark's exploits have brought him notoriety.

Questions were raised in the Houses of Parliament on several occasions about Mark benefiting from his mother's position. It has been suggested that he benefited financially directly from her dealings, most notably with Saudi Arabia in 1985, in which a million-pound Chelsea house was bought for him in 1987 by a middleman in the deal. Questions were also asked about his involvement in representing a company called Cementation that was building a university in Oman at the time that Margaret Thatcher was encouraging the Omanis to buy British.

Later Mark was arrested in South Africa for his involvement with the 2004 Equatorial Guinea coup d'état attempt. He pleaded guilty to breaking anti-mercenary legislation and was fined SAR3,000,000, and received a four-year suspended prison sentence, claiming he did not know the real nature of the expedition and had thought he was investing in a plane to run an air ambulance service for impoverished Africans. However, his co-accused, Simon Mann, claims Mark knew exactly what the money was for and was excited by the prospect of making money from it.

Carol has always regarded herself as second best in her mother's eyes. She acknowledges that there was intense competition between her and Mark, and that she has behaved well because of his "appalling" behaviour. She did this to protect her mother from the accusation that having two such wayward children would suggest that it was Mrs Thatcher who was awful and who promoted this behaviour in her favourite child.

Carol and Mark were never particularly close, but were spurred on to greater competition because of their twin relationship and the lack of an age gap between them. She felt she was not good enough for her parents. But she did feel that Mark's misdemeanours put him in the spotlight as the "embarrassing relative", leaving her to bask in the slot of "good one".

Carol was more successful academically than Mark, and she trained as a journalist at University College London. She has written several books. Carol has had a successful career as a journalist and TV personality. Although rather better liked than her twin brother, she alienated her viewers by a racist comment about a tennis player, and her refusal to understand why it was offensive or to apologise for it.

She had a high-profile relationship with Jonathan Aitken, but apparently he upset Carol by ending the relationship, and Margaret Thatcher then denied him a ministerial job. Carol has never married but has lived with a boyfriend in Switzerland. Carol and Mark have had little contact since their mother's funeral, and the animosity between them has become entrenched. They dislike each other, and Carol is particularly contemptuous of Mark.

Carol and Mark Thatcher are in a rivalrous twinship in which they have taken up opposite "sides"—the bad boy and the good girl. It is apparent that favouritism has exacerbated the tensions between them and this may be a factor common to many twins in relation to their parents. It is usually a more fluctuating situation as each of the twins moves in or out of favour. When it becomes entrenched, as in this case, the damage to the twins is more profound.

Angela and **Maria Eagle** were the first twins to be elected to Parliament. They were both junior ministers in the Labour government and then sat in the shadow cabinet. They are now both in the new shadow cabinet, Maria being shadow secretary of state for culture, media, and sport, with Angela as shadow business secretary and first secretary of state.

Angela is also the first female MP to announce publicly that she was lesbian. She became an MP in 1992, but it was only when her twin Maria was elected in May 1997, the same year that Angela announced her sexual orientation, that the Eagle twins attracted media attention.

As Decca Aitkenhead wrote in the *Guardian* (April 2011):

> They were never going to compete for the limelight amid all the peacocking psychodramas and spin of the New Labour years—and any sibling intrigue there might be between them was spectacu-larly eclipsed by the Miliband brothers' bitter fight to the top. And now that glamorous Old Etonians are back in charge of the coun-try, the sisters' understated style—quiet, self-effacing and serious-minded to the point of stodgy—might have consigned them to the background for good.

They were both given shadow cabinet briefs under Ed Miliband, Angela as shadow chief secretary to the treasury, Maria as shadow transport secretary and were the first sisters to sit around a Labour cabinet table together. They seldom gave joint interviews, and were more interested in debating a policy than talking about themselves.

Although they are DZ twins and don't really resemble each other, people frequently confuse them. Apparently they sound so alike that it is sometimes impossible to tell them apart on hearing their voices. "When I first got to parliament," says Maria, "most people thought I was coming back. All the police officers thought I'd already been here, loads of MPs thought I was a returning MP, people just didn't realise I was new—so they kept wondering why I didn't know where to go." (ibid.)

Maria explains: "People only see similarities in twins. When they know you're a twin they don't see the differences, they just see the similarities, so it was a bit of an odd introduction to parliament—people kept asking me how to do things, and I kept having to say I didn't know." (ibid.) Angela agrees with this and says people would frequently come up to her and insist on talking to her about transport policy. They were embarrassed about their mistake, but the Eagle twins are used to it.

They deny being competitive towards each other, though they are competitive outside the twin relationship. But Angela admitted she had always used the fact that she is slightly older than Maria (by fifteen minutes), though she has tried to mitigate her view on this as she has got older. "But it mattered a lot when we were kids," laughs Maria. "I mean, she got the top bunk because of that!" So we see a running undercurrent in the twinship of competition that neither likes to acknowledge.

The twin sisters shared a bedroom until the age of eighteen, when they both left home to study PPE at Oxford. They went to different colleges because they didn't want to be competing against each other for the same place. They each chose colleges that had only recently gone co-ed, to prove that women were just as good at it as men. They had always played chess and cricket and were great proponents of equality for women.

Maria graduated in 1983 to become a lawyer so she could get into politics. Angela worked for a trade union before being elected to parliament in 1992. Five years later, Maria won a parliamentary seat and they both sat in parliament together. In 2009 Angela was Minister of State for Pensions and Ageing, and Maria was Minister of State at the Ministry of Justice and the Equalities Office; they were the highest-achieving twins in British political history. The *Daily Mirror* suggested: "In fact, you might even call them Twinisters." "Twinisters, well that's a new one," Angela says. "Usually, it's 'the Eagles have landed'."

They are ideologically similar and they say they haven't had a proper row in decades. They are aware of the pull of the twin relationship but also the differences between them, an obvious one being their sexual orientation.

Thus it would appear that Angela and Maria Eagle have a well-balanced twin relationship alongside their individual relationships. Although they have followed common paths, each has developed and maintained her individuality, and they treat confusions between them with the humour borne both of an understanding of themselves and others, and of maturity.

Twins sharing power

Jaroslaw and **Lech Kaczynski** were MZ twins who governed Poland. They were very alike in appearance and political views, and rarely appeared in public together. Jaroslaw and Lech Kaczynski rose to the heights of political power in 2005. The right-wing Law and Justice Party, headed by Jaroslaw Kaczynski, won the greatest number of seats in parliamentary elections. Their views encompassed a promise of anti-gay legislation, a return to the death penalty, and a ban on abortion even for rape victims. They promised to curb free-market policies and redistribute wealth.

The twin brothers reached an agreement that party's leader, Jaroslaw, would not stand for election as Prime Minister, as they were hoping that Lech would win the presidential election to be held later that year. Lech did win the presidential election, and initially he installed someone else to be Prime Minister. However, in the summer of 2006, Lech selected Jaroslaw as Prime Minister of Poland, alongside his own presidential position. Apparently Lech did not attend Jaroslaw's inauguration ostensibly to avoid confusion amongst the press.

Jaroslaw and Lech Kaczynski were born in 1949, Jaroslaw being the elder by forty-five minutes. As children, the handsome and intelligent Kaczynski twins starred in a popular Polish children's film, *The Two Who Stole the Moon*, in 1962. They went on to study law before they became involved in the Polish anti-communist movement, prior to the collapse of communism brought about under the leadership of Lech Walesa. As adults, they spoke to each other at least ten times a day on the telephone and never made a decision without consulting each other.

There was considerable concern about so much power being in the hands of two men who were so very close. But, as Lech said, "we do have different temperaments. My brother has the temperament of a state activist and he is excellent in this role." The fact that they were twins made them better known, and that was felt to be in Poland's interests.

Jaroslaw is a bachelor and prefers solitude to high society. While Prime Minister, he lived at the official state residence with his mother and cat. He did not have a bank account and his salary was paid in cash in an envelope. Jaroslaw is regarded as the most powerful figure in democratic Poland, a political genius imbued with an intense self-belief.

Lech was married and had a daughter. He was regarded as more outgoing and confident than Jaroslaw, and as a moderating influence on his more impulsive, politically aggressive twin brother. Lech died in an aeroplane crash in 2010, in thick fog, as they were landing in Russia. Jaroslaw did not accept that the crash was an accident and blamed his political enemies for the tragedy. He refused to visit the site of the crash because he considered the Russians his enemies. Shortly after the crash he announced that he intended to succeed his late brother as the next President of Poland—a campaign he then lost.

Jaroslaw seems not to have been able to mourn the loss of his twin brother, and has instead blocked any grieving processes by frantic campaigning activity. He said he felt obliged to fulfil his brother's legacy. He visits Lech's grave every Saturday, attends a memorial ceremony every month outside the Presidential Palace, and he visits Lech's tomb in Krakow on the seventeenth of every month, the date of Lech's funeral. He has said he will be in mourning for the rest of his life, and he is always dressed in formal black clothes.

With the Kaczynski twins we see a very close twinship, but one in which their rivalry and ambitions are managed between them to allow them to reach their own political ambitions.

Much has also been made in the press of **Jenna** and **Barbara Bush**, the twin daughters of President George W. and Laura Bush. Although successful women in their own right, they are often referred to just as "the Bush twins", as the media lock into the stereotype of twins always primarily as a pair, perpetuating the idea that what is interesting about them is the twinship rather than their individuality and personal careers and successes.

Twins in restaurants

The last place one would expect to do a visual double take is at the superb London restaurant, Le Gavroche. It is eminently sedate, perfectly run, and the food is sublime. But working there are the so-called "Ginger Gemini"—**Ursula** and **Silvia Perberschlager**. These MZ twins were born in Austria, and are an important part of the Le Gavroche front of house team. They have worked at the restaurant since 2001. Silvia and Ursula both hold the position Maître d'hôtel and are well known to the regular customers, who often say that they can only tell them apart because Silvia wears a Le Gavroche pin, whilst Ursula does not. With matching extravagant red hair dye, matching statement glasses, and matching mismatched earrings, they provide the exhilarating experience of the uncanny in an otherwise sedate place.

The shock of the double is used as an engaging device that is both unsettling and intriguing.

There was a restaurant in New York, which opened in 1994, where the owners and all employees were MZ twins. Their motto was: "You can only make a first impression once; we make it twice."

The Twins Restaurant was owned by MZ twin sisters **Lisa** and **Debbie Ganz**, and actor Tom Berenger. It was staffed entirely by thirty-seven sets of MZ twins who worked the same shift, in the same station, in the same uniform. Everything was themed for multiples—twin towers, double door knobs, Doublemint gum, double-sided business cards, double light fixtures, double mirrors, and double bar stools. Twins and greater multiples got two drinks for the price of one.

They invited people to "come in for dinner and enjoy the 'Twinergy' of Twins Restaurant". Sadly it closed and has not been re-opened.

However, in the wake of its closure, there is controversy.

A restaurant has opened in Moscow called Twin Stars and, like its predecessor, it is staffed entirely by twins. Lisa Ganz has complained that Twin Stars has stolen their concept. She rather contemptuously also claims that Twin Stars only employs DZ (fraternal) twins. The owner, Alexei Khodorkovsky, disagrees. He says that diners at the Twin Stars in Moscow are treated to double attention at their tables, from MZ twins, and get a two-for-one deal. The restaurant claims to be the only one of its kind in the world, taking its inspiration from the 1964 Soviet film, *Kingdom of Crooked Mirrors*, in which a girl enters an alternate reality where she has a twin.

Again we find that the excitement about twins is exploited in terms of the visual doubling and also by favouring twins and other multiples as if to elevate their status in the world.

Media twins

David and **Frederick Barclay** are the elusive, powerful twin brothers who own the island of Brecqhou, off the coast of Sark in the Channel Islands. They have substantial business interests and are executives in the media, property, and retail sectors. The Barclays are often called "reclusive", though people close to them insist they are gregarious and personable. They avoid publicity, and access to their castle on their private island is extremely limited. Any internet search refers to them as "The Barclay brothers" and little personal information about them is available.

They were born in Hammersmith to Scottish Catholic parents, Frederick and Beatrice, and have eight siblings. Their father died when they were twelve years old, and they left school at sixteen to work in the accounts department at the General Electric Company before setting up as painters and decorators. The twins tried different business ventures before teaming up in the 1960s to redevelop old boarding houses that they converted into hotels. They continued to develop their interests in a variety of businesses, including breweries and casinos in the late 1960s. In 1995, as they became even more successful, they bought the Ritz Hotel in London's Piccadilly.

The foundation of their current empire was the Ellerman shipping, property, and brewing business, which they bought in 1983. In the 1990s they became interested in newspapers, and bought *The Scotsman*, *The European* and *Sunday Business*. *The European* closed in 1998. They bought the Telegraph Media Group amidst fierce competition and controversy about Conrad Black's shares in the company. The eldest son of Sir David Barclay (Aidan Barclay) was put in charge of Telegraph Media Group in 2004. He oversees the day-to-day running of the *Daily Telegraph*, *Sunday Telegraph*, Telegraph.co.uk and also another part of the Barclays' publishing empire, *The Spectator*, but keeps a low profile and is discreet about the influence he exerts.

The Barclay twins have run many businesses together and have together achieved considerable business success. They have both married: in 1955 David married Zoe Newton, and in the mid-1970s Frederick met and married Hiroko Asada. The brothers have four children, the eldest of whom is Aidan.

The Barclay twins are involved in philanthropy and were knighted in 2000 for their support for medical research, to which they have donated an estimated forty million pounds between 1987 and 2000. They are self-made tycoons from humble beginnings, and they are fiercely protective of their privacy.

There are a number of controversies involving the Barclay twin brothers, such as accusations that they are tax exiles, since their official residence is in Monaco but they operate most of their business in England and spend most of their time here. There have also been disputes with the government of Sark and the status of the inhabitants of Sark in relation to inheritance tax and human rights laws.

We know little of their relationship with each other, or how their families function with each other on the island, but it is striking that in the available photographs of them, they dress alike.

Performing twins

Twins who use their twinship for performance and celebrity

John and **Edward Grimes** are MZ twins who have made their name by performing as a twin team, known professionally as Jedward, an amalgamation of their names. They are an Irish singing and television-presenting duo that make their twinship central to their performances. It is pretty clear that neither of them would currently make it solo, so their twinship and a sort of weirdness has become their trademark.

They talk for each other and each regards the other twin as a copy of himself. They are rarely apart and claim the longest absence has probably been a day, but during that time they telephoned each other frequently. They are very dependent on each other for company and value each other's opinions above all others. They share a bedroom at home and sleep in bunk beds.

Thus we can see that John and Edward are twins who are entwined both in their professional performances, and also lead a deeply enmeshed twin relationship in their personal lives.

The MZ twins **Liesbeth** and **Angelique Raeven** are potent examples of an enmeshed and crippling twin relationship from which neither can escape. They were born in 1971 in Heerlen, in the Netherlands. They work together as performance artists and collaborate under the name L. A. Raeven. L. A. stands for Liesbeth and Angelique, so like Jedward, they perform together under one name. The focus of their art is their bodies and they call it "aesthetic terrorism", as it is directed at the perceived images of themselves. They focus on two aspects of themselves: their extreme thinness is used to address the way the fashion industry portrays ideal women as super-thin; and their twinship and similarity in appearance is used to draw attention to the way twins are perceived as "cute". They maintain and use their extreme thinness and their enmeshed twin relationship to draw attention to these factors.

It is difficult to discern what belongs to their own pathology and what is created for their art to draw attention to thinness and twinship as seen by others. Although both twins are unnaturally thin, they become angry at the idea that they are anorexic. Nevertheless, they engage in compelling eating rituals, keeping themselves emaciated to the point of being unhealthy/ill, and making sure neither one eats more than the other. They are locked in the fact that they are twins, and seem to be unable to move out of the enclosed twin relationship into one that would allow them more separateness and individuality, and normal lives.

In their late teens they separated for six years. Angelique worked as an assistant to the fashion designer Jean-Paul Gaultier, while Liesbeth became a nurse, and then went into the art world. The fashion world is notorious for its ultra-thin women and Angelique would have felt quite in place amongst them. In contrast, Liesbeth felt she became healthy at that time and she gained weight, looking more normal. However, she felt so unhappy that she left and was reunited with Angelique in the twin relationship. With the twinship restored, she felt more at ease. She feels there is no friend or lover to whom she could feel as close as she does to Angelique.

Thus, their attempts to create separate lives and careers failed, they say, because people still treated them as one person. Apparently they gave up the attempt to live separate lives in order to try to prove contradictorily that they were two individuals—an odd idea given that they now perform under one name and use their "freakishness" as grossly underweight twins, together weighing what one person would weigh, to prove this.

"We were so irritated by this twin image, but after ten years of suffering, you know you are denying yourself what you really want [a telling phrase]. But you still feel: 'Are they interested in me because I'm a twin or because I'm interesting?'" says Liesbeth. Angelique agrees. "After ten years, we knew we had to do something to make our views clear, and it was more fruitful than working alone." (Quotes taken from videos and discussion on their website, no longer available.)

Like the Gibbons twins, Liesbeth and Angelique are engaged in a life-death struggle with each other in an attempt to deal with their impossibly enmeshed twinship. Their first important video installation (2001) was called You Are Me and it was based on the true story of the silent British twin sisters June and Jennifer Gibbons. Like the Gibbons twins, they both long for separateness but also fear it. They seem to be so entwined that the only way out would be the death of one, yet that would also feel like the death of the other. They watch each other intensely and move almost in synchrony. They believe that being twins gives them more power, and they are committed to being in total control over each other and their viewers.

Their videos reflect how they feel bound in their love-hate twinship. Liesbeth and Angelique Raeven exemplify an enmeshed state. They seem neither to be able to live harmoniously together, nor to separate and live apart. Together they support each other through a mix of love and hate, and it seems that their anorexic eating rituals bind them in a deadly relationship that offers no hope of development, but also keeps them both alive—just.

Some of this is reflected in their art videos, as when one seems to be trying to drown the other while swimming. Neither seems to have achieved the awareness of separateness that would be necessary for the development of individual selves and lives, and for the acknowledge-ment of loss necessary to mourn either their enmeshed togetherness or the death of one of them. Without a greater degree of separation between them, mourning would not be possible. They live in a stultify-ing world, making an art form of it, but this art seems to be rooted in a perverse depiction of life in an enmeshed twinship rather than based on creativity. Despite their wish to depict themselves as "terrorists" against the desirable images of thin women and twins as cute, they treat their twinship and their extreme thinness like a fetish, to be admired, longed for, bound to, perhaps worshipped. Like any fetish, it does not provide an opportunity for growth and development. Rather, it binds the indi-viduals in a deathly embrace.

Liesbeth and Angelique are obsessed with their sense of identity and this led to quite dramatic events a few years ago when one of them, Angelique, became so malnourished that she almost died and had been sectioned by the authorities to save her life. When Angelique was taken into hospital, Liesbeth was so stricken with the loss of her twin sister she too felt as if she was dying. As a result of Angelique's malnour-ishment, her bones became fragile and her spine fractured. She is now eight centimetres (almost three inches) shorter than she used to be. After this Angelique thought she was ugly and she did not want to work with Liesbeth the way she used to. This affected their working relationship.

Angelique and Liesbeth live together, and have done so for some years in what they describe as a symbiotic relationship. Their earlier attempts at separation always ended up in dramas of one kind or another. They do everything together and since the earlier hospitalisation of Angelique with severe malnourishment, they are closely monitored by doctors.

Their strange, almost synchronised, behaviour is as disturbing as their stick-thin physical appearance. The twin sisters refer to themselves as "twins gone bad". Their enclosed twin world involves and is maintained by rituals and constant tiny power struggles that they publicise and call their art. Angelique states "Together we are strong and in harmony, apart we are like only half a person."

One of their newer art pieces, called Mindless Living, reflects how enmeshed their twinship is. As quoted on their website:

> In their work they question and critique the idealized images of women advocated by the mass media. L. A. Raeven displays the downside of the norms and values shown by these images. They demonstrate, in a way close to self-harm, the often thin line existing between being ideal or distorted ... The exhibition Mindless Living presents two symbioses next to each other. In Mindless Living I the symbiosis in which L. A. Raeven has lived for years is shown by an installation consisting of a circular chair with a hypnotic film for adults.

Liesbeth then had a baby (the paternity and details of this are not disclosed) and they have prepared a second art installation, now reflecting the symbiotic relationship between Liesbeth and her baby. She says she suddenly and unexpectedly found herself pregnant and they found this beautiful. This new work on symbiotic relationships is entitled Mindless Living II. In it the baby will be placed in a womb-like cot with smells, consistency, and sounds reflecting those of the womb, so the baby will feel it is back in the womb, still unborn.

Again from their website:

> With the new installation Mindless Living II, L. A. Raeven wants to conclude their former symbiosis and start a new one: the symbiosis between mother and child. Normally, this symbiosis has a positive meaning, but in Mindless Living II it is carried on too far. In the installation the baby is reminded of his time in the womb. While lying in the womb cradle the baby will be brought into a minor

trance, hearing a text which is undermining his confidence in order to stay in a symbiosis with his mother. The baby will be influenced in everything, preventing him from finding his own way. As a result the baby wants to stay in the safe warm place of the womb.

Mindless Living II shows the friction between letting go and protecting a child, in which a healthy balance needs to be found in order to mature into a happy and independent individual.

So they write as if they understand the malfunction that they are trying to illuminate, but seem unable to actually deal with these issues in themselves.

This installation reflects not only the usual tensions as a baby develops into its own person, but also the experience of the womb-like twinship where both Liesbeth and Angelique remain unborn as individuals, and the way their lack of personal development has affected their view of the baby. It is as if the baby is no more than an extension of Liesbeth and must be the same as her, as the twinship has been projected into the baby and she twins with her baby.

Both these works reflect the difficulties these twins face in finding and leading separate lives, their lack of growth and development as individuals, and their clinging to this state. Likewise it seems that they hope Liesbeth's baby will be kept bound to his mother instead of becoming a separate independent person. They feel utterly bound in their stifling twin relationship but cling to it as they fear that separateness would endanger their lives, would arouse the fear of annihilation that is expressive of primitive, unformed states of mind where boundaries are too porous to enable the individual to have a sense of being safe in her own skin, a sense of self that is not totally dependent on a twin or mother.

Thus their latest works, as the early ones, exemplify an enmeshed, deathly twin relationship that prevents growth and development. They seem to hope that they will free themselves and others from the crippling conditions in which they find themselves through their focus on the stifling, sometimes unbearable psychological closeness of their twin relationship and the dynamics between them, and on their emaciated bodies. The trouble is that they talk the talk without exhibiting the maturity and emotional intelligence that would enable them to start finding a way of life as individuals outside the crippling twinship and its compulsively competitive non-eating/self-starvation.

They have claimed to be artists challenging our aesthetic values. If art represents a symbolic transformation of internal processes, then in contrast, L. A. Raeven could be seen as concretising their difficulties by making a display of their anorexic eating rituals, mindless art works, and their deadly, enmeshed twin relationship.

The Romanian-born pair of twin sisters **Gabriela** and **Monica Irimia**, were a British-based pop duo known as The Cheeky Girls. Their success, however, became a trap in which they became anorexic. The Cheeky Girls lost control of their lives and this led them both to suffer from eating disorders. They secretly starved themselves to six and a half stone each, and caused permanent damage to themselves including arthritis in their spines and knees, ruined digestive systems, and kidney stones. They weighed everything they ate and survived on soft drinks. They lived alone in London or in a hotel when touring, but they became so frightened of food that they didn't leave the house in case they came into contact with food.

Much of their appeal rested on their being two cheeky twins. Their performance was based on their "identical" twinship in an idealisation of twins that severely limited their individual development.

Performers who happen to be twins

Twin brothers **Robin** and **Maurice Gibb** formed the band The Bee Gees with their older brother, Barry. Both Gibb twins, who were born in 1949 on the Isle of Man, have now died. Maurice, the younger by thirty-five minutes, died in January 2003 following complications during intestinal surgery. Robin died in May 2012 after a long battle with cancer. Robin reportedly spoke of Maurice as he lay dying, saying, "I wish Mo was here, I can't believe he is gone." (Grossman, 2013)

While the twin relationship between Robin and Maurice was not played upon by them or the press, the intensity of their twin bond was expressed by Robin after Maurice died. Their elder brother, Barry, recalled the decade of separation that Robin endured after Maurice died. At Robin's funeral he said, "When you're twins, you're twins for life … You go through every emotion. And they're finally together. I think the greatest pain for Robin in the past ten years was losing his twin brother, and I think it did all kinds of things to him."

As a good example of our fascination with twins, the fact that **Elvis Presley** had a twin who died at birth has spawned reams of written and unwritten fantasies about the effect this had on Elvis's life. Not only are there those who believe Elvis himself is still alive, there are some who claim his twin Jesse is alive and living somewhere remote hidden from view—another Elvis to idolise.

Apparently Elvis's twin brother Jesse (first-born) was born dead and the family have recounted stories about their surprise at the emergence of a second live baby. Elaine Dundy (1985) wrote a biography of Elvis and his mother. In it, we can see both the idealisation of twins and the idealisation of Elvis Presley, and it also illustrates the reality of the enduring nature of the twin relationship in the internal world.

> Elvis was born a twin … The fact that the mystery of death was attendant at his birth, that the very beginning of his life marked the end of his brother's, affected him throughout his life in a way that people who are not twins would find hard to understand. (Dundy, 1985, p. 67)

It is likely that the fact that he was a twin would have influenced Elvis as he developed, as discussed in Chapter Four. The residual sensate memories Elvis would have had of his twin in utero, and the birth stories told by his parents and family, would certainly have enhanced his sense of himself as a lone twin.

Elvis's middle name was Aron, while that of his dead twin was Garon. (It is another feature of our fascination with twins that they are so often given very similar or rhyming names.) There are many suggestions that Elvis was deeply lonely and always looking for his twin, or a twin-like substitute. He was very attached to his mother, as was she to him, as if they had twinned with each other.

Larry Geller, once Elvis's hairdresser, claims Elvis was always aware of his twin, spoke to him, and suffered guilty feelings about being alive while Jesse died. He suggests that Jessie may have been the force behind Elvis's creativity and self-destructive tendencies. This gets further mythologised into the idea that Elvis was never able to overcome the death of his brother, and his brother's death may have eventually led to Elvis's death, so he could be reunited with his brother in the afterlife. Strong emphasis is placed on the unbearable longing of lone twins.

Another performer whose twin died at birth was **Liberace**, and as with Elvis Presley, there have been claims that he was always searching for a twin substitute. What these stories tell us is that we believe that being born a twin, whether or not both babies survive, will have a lasting effect on our personality and development. We also learn about our own need to construct stories about lost twins and loneliness, and ideas about the sources of our creativity in this lifelong search for a perfect soulmate.

Literary twins

Playwrights **Peter** and **Anthony Shaffer** are twins who have both been extremely successful in creating literary works for the theatre and film. They were born in 1926 and were both educated at St Paul's. After three years of non-military service in the coal mines of Kent and Yorkshire they both went to study at Cambridge.

Peter became one of England's most popular and respected playwrights. He wrote three mystery novels together with Anthony, under the pseudonym Peter Anthony.

In 1958 Peter Shaffer had his first great theatrical success with *Five Finger Exercise*, and he had other notable successes with *The Royal Hunt of the Sun, Equus*, and *Amadeus*. "His plays traverse the centuries and the globe, raising questions that have perplexed minds from Job to Samuel Beckett." (Benedict Nightingale in the *New York Times*)

Anthony Shaffer was born five minutes earlier than Peter. After studying at Cambridge he became a barrister. Peter, who was already writing plays, was horrified when his twin brother Anthony left a career as a barrister to write the hit play *Sleuth*.

The intense rivalry about the family name was a subject often seen in the brothers' plays. Peter, in unpublished letters written in the 1960s, revealed his obsessive jealousy over "the name thing", as he repeatedly begged Anthony to publish his plays under a pseudonym. Having already established himself as a playwright, Peter feared that Anthony was about to trample on his territory. He wrote:

> I realise that all my life, until I was 32, I felt anonymous, feeble, unemployable, never an individual ... I suppose a lot of it had to do with being a twin. One of "the boys". Never quite unique ... Now, in some hateful way ... I do feel threatened. As if my little Kingdom

has been invaded, and I am no longer to be The Playwright, but again part of that faintly cute and annihilating "Which one of them did it?" (*Guardian*, 2007)

In another passage, he implored: "Before it's too late ... I beg you to take another name for writing—make a Self which everyone will know as you—a glittering persona you can develop throughout the years. I will be Me; you will be You." (ibid.)

Anthony, who died in 2001, rejected Peter's pleas to write under a pseudonym and continued to use the family name. He was nominated for an Oscar for the film version of *Sleuth* and wrote screenplays for the Alfred Hitchcock film *Frenzy* and for *The Wicker Man*.

Peter was annoyed that the *New York Post* had wrongly credited him with *Anyone for Murder*. He wrote: "It threw me into a sort of tizz ... Let me spit it out, since it is ... eating me ... I feel in some horrid way threatened. I'm vain, I know. I quite like having my first name dropped in references to me, and am distressed if, to distinguish us, it has to be put back again." Despite these rivalries, Sir Peter and Anthony spoke most days by phone.

After Anthony's death, Peter gave an interview to *The Times* (*Guardian*, 2001) in which he spoke about his dead brother, as he prepared to bring to the London stage Anthony's play *Murderer*. "I was very depressed by Tony's death, and distressed, and in some ways have remained so."

The intense rivalry within the twin relationship is very evident in their letters and their literary works. Peter's desperate wish to be seen as an individual, not just a twin, is a potent factor in their rivalry and it seems to be a rather fragile internal structure. The intense loneliness when one twin dies is also evident in the Shaffer twins.

CHAPTER FIVE

Twins around the world: mythology, beliefs, and cultural practices

In the last chapter we looked at the excitement about, and fascination with, the twin relationship generated by our feelings of intrigue about the existence of twins and what they represent of our own internal longings, but through our idealisation of "celebrities". The frenzy aroused by the media, and in some cases used by the famous or infamous twins themselves, indicates the perceived intensity and magic of the twin bond in some twin pairs. In this chapter, I will look at some other aspects of the disturbance aroused by twins and the enactments that are consequent upon this arousal, and the beliefs on which they are based.

I have already written about our fascination with twins linked with our unconscious phantasies about ourselves and the impact this has on intimate relationships. In the wider world, the perceptions of twins and the consequent treatment of twins at birth are based on myths and legends linked with belief systems and religions. These systems are used to create a coherent narrative about the apparently strange and exciting phenomenon of twins, to try to deal with their supposed magical powers or the threat they are felt to pose to society.

Beliefs about the meaning of the birth of twins vary greatly as do the ritual practices relating to these beliefs. On the one hand we may encounter the celebration of the birth of twins accompanied by what appear to be the rather poetic and charming rituals and beliefs surrounding the birth of twins, all over the world; and on the other, we find the dark side, rituals in which the twins and sometimes the mother of the twins are banished or killed. As I will explore later, the idealisation of twins, and the denigration and sometimes murderous fear of twins, represent two sides of the coin, both of which avoid the reality of the real nature of twinship and the birth of twins.

Twins feature prominently in myths and legends, and the cultural practices relating to twins throughout the world are based on the local beliefs about twin birth. These beliefs and the myths created to explain the twin birth reflect not only our fascination with twins and the dynamics of twinning, but also the anxiety or excitement associated with the birth of two babies at about the same time. Myths may tell various stories, but those about twin gods or the twin children of gods are found throughout the world.

The prominence of twins in folklore, in myths, legends, bible stories and so on, and the common attribution of godlike or demonic status to one of them, indicates the importance and the deep ethnic roots of our fascination with twins; and the associated beliefs surmount superficial curiosity. As symbols, twins offer a natural and available representation of the inner tensions we all experience, and also the discordance between people, and between the forces of nature and human beings. Twins in stories, myths, and legends may be used to represent the extremes of personal fears and experience, and the powerful forces active in our relationships, as well as intergenerational and international dynamics.

Among the themes about twins that are expressed in myths and legends is a commonly expressed idea that twins are two halves of one being, as often expressed in literature (see Chapter Six) and in many cultural practices. In everyday life, the almost automatic question asked when encountering twins is "are they identical?" whether the twins look alike and are even of different sexes. I believe this question originates in our own longings for a perfect soulmate and our projection of this longing onto the two babies we see before us. It will also represent the longing in each of the twins for the ideal twin. The question is relevant biologically to monozygotic twins where the fertilised egg has actually split to create two foetuses. However, dizygotic twins also commonly have a sense of some aspects of shared identity, as if they too are the result of a similar process of splitting. When alone, twins often experience a feeling of incompleteness, as if something essential is missing. They feel lonely, and yearn for a lost part of the self. I have explored the roots of this experience in Chapter Two.

Ritual practices around the world relating to the substitution or reparation to the twin for an unmanageable loss if the other twin has died, are linked with the belief that twins are two parts of one whole. As we saw in Chapter Three, where one twin dies, the surviving twin's sense of longing and loss can be overwhelming, and there are many accounts of endless waiting and longing to be reunited with the lost twin. So ritual practices to compensate the twin for her loss would be based on our understanding of the severity of the loss for the twin, and our own fears of loss of part of the self through bereavement, exacerbated by a belief that twins are gods or demons and that the loss will generate impossible anger and damage.

The theme of rivalry in twin legends is a very common one. Rivalry between twins may often be very intense and a combination of the extreme closeness and rivalrous feelings between them complicates their sense of oneness within their relationship. Where the rivalry and violence is directed outwards, twins work together against the external enemy. Mythical twins are commonly portrayed as engaged in fighting and war, and they battle together against a common enemy. One twin may experience an expression of violence towards the other twin as an experience of a violent act against the self. Mythical twins are often heartbroken when the other twin has been hurt and hasten to their rescue. When a mythical twin dies, the survivor longs to be reunited with the dead twin and may appeal to the gods to achieve this.

What are myths, legends, and bible stories? Myths represent universal phantasies, stories we create to express, and to understand and resolve, our unconscious processes and hidden conflicts. They are found in various forms in many cultures and belief systems. Myths are symbolic representations of our experience as we develop psychically from the dependency of our infancy towards our separateness as adults, and as we develop communities and nations. In the process of myth creation, unconscious aspects of the psyche are projected onto legendary figures in stories, myths, the bible, and so on, about the birth and evolution of mankind, and the coming into being of the psychological self, the creation of nations and national identity. Mythical figures are thus representatives of our internal world and relationships, a historical memory of universal phantasies and struggles. They are so enduring and compelling because they represent our unconscious fantasies.

Sigmund Freud described myths and fairy tales as "the products of ethnic imagination" (Freud, 1912–1913, p. 185). Levi-Strauss (1955) referred to myths as dynamic tales that explain the past, the present, and the future. Myths are a narrative way of organising and making sense of human experience and are used to try to master the unknown. The stories become embellished and coloured as they are passed down through the generations.

I will explore several myths in which splitting or the creation of a double is central, and in which the creation of mythical twins elucidates the processes involved in development and twinning, as well as in the evolution of mankind. The creation of two from one, or of two figures representing different aspects of one, is a common theme in mythology. Stories of the creation of mankind are centred on such splitting, the creation of man and woman, of a double, of twin-like first beings, or gods and goddesses. The relationship between the twins, the bonds or disturbances, is expressed in the myths, and represents our internal struggle for intimacy, closeness, and love, as well as the hatred, unease, envy, and jealousy that exists within actual relationships and for personal as well as group, tribal, and national boundaries.

Creation myths

Plato (360 BCE) wrote about the nature of love: Aristophanes proposed that the original nature of man was not as we now know it. Instead, a being of double nature, with two heads, four arms, and four legs was split into two to create two halves that became a man and a woman. The reason for this split is that these double beings were terribly strong and so confident, they tried to attack the gods. Zeus decided to humble them and teach them manners by reducing their power, by cutting them in two. In this way their strength would be diminished and their numbers increased. This also served another purpose as these beings made offerings to the gods, so splitting them in two would make them more profitable to the gods, thus doubling their value.

After Zeus halved them, he healed their wounds and in this humiliated, vulnerable state, the two halves found that they each longed for and desired the other half. On coming together again, the two halves embraced and were so eager to grow into one again, that they would have died of hunger rather than separate. If one half died, the other half sought another mate to cling to. Zeus rescued them from this difficulty by adjusting their genitalia so that they could breed by sowing their seed in one another, in an embrace, rather than on the ground like grasshoppers. So, according to this myth, our desire for one another was founded in a wish to regain our original nature, making one of two. Each one, when separated, is but a half and is always looking for the other half, like lost twin souls.

Explaining the nature of love, Aristophanes stated:

> And when one of them finds his other half ... the pair are lost in an amazement of love and friendship and intimacy, and one will not be out of the other's sight ... even for a moment: these are they who pass their lives with one another; yet they could not explain what they desire of one another. For the intense yearning which each of them has towards the other does not appear to be the desire of intercourse, but of something else which the soul desires and can not tell, and of which she has only a dark and doubtful presentiment ... human nature was originally one and we were a whole, and the desire and pursuit of the whole is called love. (Plato, 360 BCE, p. 722)

Thus he also expresses the longing felt by all of us for something lost that we once had, and the yearning felt by twins when they are apart—an experience that is particularly acute because of their deep sensate bond.

It is often assumed that twins, especially MZ twins, share a personality and are like Plato's creatures that originate from one egg that splits. The notion that twins share a personality is a fallacy but they may deal with their rivalry by distributing personality traits between them, reflecting the idea of oneness split into two bodies.

Similar longings can be seen in the biblical creation myth that is the traditional story of **Adam** and **Eve**. The omnipotent, omniscient God of Genesis created two beings who became the parents of the human race. Initially, like Plato's creatures they were bound together as one. On the sixth day of the creation of the world, God created man (*ish*, in Hebrew) in his own image, out of the dust of the earth (*adamah*), and breathed life into his nostrils. He then put Adam into a deep sleep, and while Adam was unconscious, he took one of Adam's ribs, closed the wound, and made the rib into a woman (*ishah*). Woman was thus created as a cloned aspect of the man, created by a split.

"And Adam said, This is now bone of my bones, and flesh of my flesh ... Therefore shall a man leave his father and his mother and cleave unto his wife; and they shall be one flesh." (Genesis, 2:23–24).

God called the woman Eve (*Chavah*, from *chai* meaning life) because she was the mother of all living. (The dual meaning of "cleave" is discussed below.)

There is, however, another story that illustrates the tensions told not in the book of Genesis, but referred to in Isaiah 34, and explained by Graves and Patai (1992). In this story Lilith was Adam's first mate, not Eve. God created Adam out of dust, and he created Lilith in the same way, except that he used filth and sediment instead of pure dust. There were severe tensions between Lilith and Adam, as Lilith refused to submit to Adam's tyrannical demands. With twin-like rivalry she claimed that, like him, she was made of dust and was therefore his equal. Adam tried to force her to obey him and, in a rage, Lilith (whose name derives from "female demon" or "wind spirit") soared up into the air. She fled to the Red Sea where she remained in isolation. Adam then complained to God that he was lonely, and God created a more compliant Eve from Adam's rib.

In this version of the story, Lilith was the first female double of the first man and we encounter the idea of one twin as a demon or a god. These two versions of this creation story indicate the internal tensions that we encounter as we try to become ourselves and relate to others. Eve represents a complementary, mature part of the self, and Lilith a deeper, more destructive shadow that is more difficult to integrate, and which may be suppressed and banished to a distant desolate place.

> Wildcats shall meet with hyenas,
> goat-demons shall call to each other;
> there too Lilith shall repose,
> and find a place to rest.
> There shall the owl nest
> and lay and hatch and brood in its shadow
>
> (Isaiah 34:14)

They represent the tensions between intimacy and separateness; between siblings as they seek to find their place in the family; between different peoples trying to forge a common identity. And they represent the way twins are often perceived as good or bad.

These two stories about the creation of men and women offer a further insight into our psychological nature. Eve gave birth to human babies, Cain and Abel, whereas Lilith bore only demons. But as was also told in the biblical story, Cain killed Abel—the murderous rivalry seen in twins, siblings, and between nations. Eve was impregnated by sex that was procreative in the normal partnered way, representing maturity, compromise, and creativity. Legend has it that Lilith tried to destroy the offspring so created. In contrast, Lilith was impregnated as a result of sex without love, without mutuality, sex for personal satisfaction only, that is masturbation and nocturnal emissions. Thus Lilith represents a part of the self that remains cut off, envious, and destructive, with an urge to destroy creative internal processes—a perverse solution we see in everyday life between people and nations.

In the traditional Adam and Eve story, we see a benign splitting of one into two, to create a couple, a pair related to each other by their difference, the first man and the first woman, Adam and Eve, in a perfect and trouble-free state of mind, the Garden of Eden. The destructive aspects later emerged in the form of the serpent, the tempter, the corrupter of pure good—representing envy, the destructive side of the self. The idealised state of mind of the Garden of Eden was thus shattered. The couple were expelled from paradise and had to face the reality of the external world, of the knowledge of good and evil, and the need to work and compromise.

The story of Adam and Lilith expresses the tension between either integrating the split aspects of the self or disowning them. The Adam and Eve story looks at the need for differentiation and separateness to maintain a realistic unity of self. This struggle is central to development in twins and the two versions of the creation myth represent both the personal struggles we all face in developing to maturity, and the additional tensions experienced by twins in their psychic growth.

The word "cleave" has dual and opposite meanings—to cleave together (to cling, to adhere) or to cleave apart (to split, or cause to split, especially along a natural weakness) (Collins English Dictionary, 2003, p. 317). Milton (*Areopagitica*, 1644, p. 13) wrote: "It was from out of the rind of one apple tasted, that the knowledge of good and evil, as Two Twins cleaving together, leaped forth into the world."

The tension between cleaving together and cleaving apart is an essential part of development, and is particularly marked in twins as they both cling together as a unit and also wish to be separate individuals.

Magical powers attributed to twins

Cultural practices reflect beliefs about the origins of twins. It is common in mythology to find twins attributed god-like status and representing magical powers.

We are all familiar with a cult of divine twins, one human and the other a god, or where both become gods. I will explore the origins of this myth. It originates from a remote antiquity, in Ancient Greece and Rome and is also found elsewhere in the world. The story Castor and Pollux is one of the well-known examples. It is often proposed that the idea of mortal or immortal twins originates in the belief that an ordinary human father can only beget one child at a time. So a second child born at the same time must be the issue of a god. The first child is considered to be mortal, the second partly divine. As a result, magical properties are attributed to both twins, for example their ability to grant victory in war, to cure disease, bring rain, calm storms, and create immunity to disease.

The legendary **Castor** and **Pollux**, the Heavenly Twins, were worshipped in Greece, Sicily, and Italy as the guardians of seafarers. They were twins who were bound by a love that obliterated any rivalry between them. The stories vary, but commonly the story tells that they were born to Leda after the god Zeus, disguised as a swan, seduced her. Leda had also conceived by her husband, Tyndareus. She gave birth to four children: Castor and Clytaemnestra, who were the children of Tyndareus (a mortal), while Pollux (also known as Polydeuces) and Helen were Zeus's children and therefore immortal.

Castor (a breaker of horses) and Pollux (a master boxer) were active in many battles. Castor was killed in battle and Pollux was so distraught that in his sorrow and loneliness he pleaded with Zeus that he should not outlive his beloved twin brother and asked to share his divinity with Castor. Zeus eventually granted this wish by allowing them to live alternately in heaven and the netherworld. As a further reward for their brotherly love, Zeus placed their images among the stars as the Twins (Gemini), the Dioscuri (sons of Zeus). They represented the ever-changing cycle of night and day, from light to dark, and dark to light, a theme found in other heroic mythical twins. Castor and Pollux became the patrons of shipwrecked sailors and were granted the power to send favourable winds after an appropriate sacrifice had been made. They are generally seen as helpers, and as saviours, and are found in some form in many polytheistic religions, as eternally bound twin gods. They are often seen as patrons of agriculture and the bestowers of rain.

Thus Castor and Pollux were twins inseparable even in death, and represent an enmeshed twinship based on narcissistic love. In contrast, Jacob and Esau were bound in a twinship of hatred, the opposite way of dealing with an over-close relationship where intimacy may feel invasive and rivalry is intense.

Heavenly twins were represented in ancient Celtic cultures. A pagan altar has been found at Notre Dame, Paris, with a dedication by the boatmen of the Seine to certain Celtic divinities, and among them the Heavenly Twins. The cult of Heavenly Twins was superseded all over Europe and the Christian East by saints who performed similar functions and are often called by similar names.

Twins are frequently given assonant names, or names that are variants of one another. The assumed sameness of twins is represented in Teutonic mythology, where twins and other multiples were all given the same name, as they were conceived together and born at the same time. The common name declares their simultaneous origin. Thus Westmar had three sons called Grep. Harald and Asa had twins called Halfdan-the-Black and Halfdan-the-White, distinguishing them by the colour of their hair. Similarly there were twin Irish priests called Heuald-the-Black and Heuald-the-White. In some cultures there is a custom of calling twins by names specifically given to each twin. The Egba sub-group of the Yoruba people in western Nigeria call all twins Taiwo (first born) and Kehinde (the one who follows or comes last); the Benga of West Africa call twins Ivaha (a wish) and Ayĕnwĕ (unseen) regardless of sex.

There are common Indo-Germanic roots for the belief in Divine Twins, the Dioscuri, the Asvins of the Rig-Veda, and the Dewa-deli of Lithuania.

The Vedic Asvins (Ashvins, Atvins, also known as the Nâsatya) of India are another pair of Divine Twins. They are the Indo-European equivalent of the Greek Dioscuri. They are often represented as two golden honey-coloured twins, divine horsemen. They ride in a golden shining chariot. They bring up the morning light of the sky by making a path through the clouds for the dawn goddess, Ushas, and they overcome darkness. They are identified as stars of morning and evening, divinities of the dawn and the evening twilight. They perform medical feats including the revival of the dead. They are doctors of the gods, friends of the sick and unfortunate, and give back youth and beauty, and are the inventors of medicines. They are inseparable companions who have a wondrous ability to correct wrongs, to reverse and negate nature, and to avert catastrophe. As divinities of light they would also have the powers to personify lightning (Zeus's weapon) and the storm. They came to be looked upon as protectors from the violence of the elements, and thence of voyagers on river or sea, and, by extension of the idea, of travellers generally. Their powers would gradually grow until they covered a still larger area of human life.

The Asvins represent the reconciliation of opposing forces by accommodation, a harmonious synthesis. Their father, Surya or Vivasvat, was the rising sun, representing righteousness and eternal law; their mother, Sanjna (Saranyu), represented consciousness or understanding. The mother was unable to stand the brilliance of her husband, and she retired to the shade, assuming the form of a mare. The father accommodated himself to her transmutation and became a stallion, and followed her to her forest retreat. Their twin children, the Asvins, combine the godlike brilliance of their father with the retiring understanding of their mother, thus enabling them to relate to man's limitations and also act as benevolent healers. They became gods after reviving and bestowing eternal youth and beauty on an old man who was married to a beautiful young woman whom they had tried lure away from him, so she would marry one of them.

Similar gods of light and dark are found in Ancient Persia, the twin gods Ohrmuzd (light) and Ahriman (dark).

We might wonder about the meaning of the duality attached to twins, as expressed in myths, legends, biblical stories, and simple everyday life—god and mortal, dark and light, the good and the bad twin, and so on. I think it has to do with the sense of the uncanny when we see twins, like seeing a double even if the form differs. When we see twin babies, children, or even adults they seem to form the idealised god-like pairing. The sense of otherness that we experience when we encounter someone who is not born at the same time, does not look so alike, and does not represent deep longings based on our earliest good experiences, is lacking. Perhaps we try to separate and differentiate them magically by attributing contrasting characteristics to them.

Amongst the earliest agricultural people, a mother who had produced twins, and the twins themselves, were regarded as especially influential in creating fertility and inducing rain from the skies to create a fertile land. From earliest times, stargazing and star naming have been a central part of religious practice. It had been observed that there was a morning star and an evening star. Hesper, the evening star, and Phosphor, the morning star, were the two sons of Eos and they represent the double aspect of the planet Venus. Phosphor was the son of Astreaus and could be seen with a torch in his hand in the guise of a winged spirit flying through the air before his mother's chariot. Hesper was the brightest star in the firmament, and was the son of Atlas. These stars were believed to be twins because one came up when the other went down. As the skies became light before the sun arose one star would disappear; the other became lost in the dark after the sun had set. It was believed that one must be immortal, the other mortal, and twins became identified with the stars. So the idea of the heavenly twins as the patrons of agriculture and the bestowers of rain originates from earlier civilisations. The evolution of the cult of heavenly twins forms part of the oldest religions in the world.

The origin of the cult of heavenly twins predates the ideas about dual paternity and originates in a time long predating Greek civilisation. Harris in 1906 examined stories about very early man and beliefs and practices in various tribes in Africa and elsewhere, as yet uninfluenced by Western culture. He told the story of an Essequibo Indian woman (of South America) who gave birth to twins. One was sickly and the *pui* man (sorcerer, witchdoctor) was called in. There was sickness in the community and he said the cause of sickness within the community was one of the twins, who was the child of Kenaima—an external soul, always harmful. One night, as an owl hooted, the sickly child cried. The *pui* man claimed the bird was the Kenaima father of the sickly twin, calling to it. The child was killed by throwing it into a pit of fire, burned alive.

Harris uses this example as "an expression of the most elementary thought of the human race on the subject of the birth of twins. The occurrence is abnormal, an abnormal cause must be found for the abnormal effect." (1906, p. 7) The hypothesis, as later continued in Greek thinking about twins, is that of dual paternity—one father is known and visible, the other is unknown and a spirit. So, with one more step we can see how Castor and Pollux, and Amphion and Zethus (see later), came to be considered to be one mortal, the other divine.

Harris postulates that the first explanation for the birth of twins was a spontaneous one, predating even that of stargazing and star naming. Before such ideas as dual paternity and stargazing and naming, twins were thought to be taboo. Tribes in West Africa were observed to kill twins and sometimes the mother too. The twins were regarded as uncanny and unnatural and were put to death. These customs were later modified in various ways. Sometimes the mother and her twins were banished, either into the fields and left to fend for themselves, or to twin villages. So the original taboo was modified from death to exile. These modifications were in both belief and custom, and over time they evolved into killing just one twin, and the belief in dual paternity, and later a belief in sky-parentage.

The origin of the idea of sky-parentage seems to be that women have always been connected with agriculture and taking care of the fertility of crops, while men hunted. Amongst the Barongo of West Africa, mothers of twins were seen as particularly fertile and productive, therefore valuable in producing a good crop and rain. Thus twins came to be connected with rain and the sky—the children of the sky, eventually the Dioscuri. When a woman gave birth to twins, the other women of the tribe would pour water over her and the twin babies as a rain charm. She was called Tilo, and they were the children of Tilo.

So we see the evolution of a cult in the oldest religions of the world from an idea that twins were uncanny, therefore taboo, through moderation of belief and practice, to the idealisation of twins as gods, as special and magical.

Twins in mythology emphasise two possible lines of development in the twin relationship. On the one hand twins have been depicted as so tied to each other in an apparently loving bond as to be unable or unwilling to survive alone, like Castor and Pollux, as explored above. On the other, the major factors are intense rivalry, violent, murderous hatred, and jealousy, as in Jacob and Esau, and in Romulus and Remus. It is interesting that mythology about twins emphasises the more imma- ture aspects of the twin relationship, rather than the mature view where there can be compromise and thoughtfulness. This is further testament to myths representing our unconscious untempered desires, emotions, and experiences.

Rivalry between twins leading to the creation of nations

The intense rivalry between twins has been expressed in several legends. **Romulus** and **Remus** were the sons of Mars and Sylvia, a vestal virgin. She was condemned to be drowned in the Tiber with her twin sons because of the ancient taboo against twins. The cradle holding the twins became stuck in reeds and the twins were found by a she-wolf who cared for and suckled the newborn babies. They were later found by a royal herdsman whose wife cared for the twin boys. Romulus and Remus planned to build a city on the banks of the Tiber. Romulus ploughed a furrow to establish the city boundary, and Remus impetuously jumped over it. Romulus killed Remus for this transgression. This deed represents the power struggle so common between twins and perhaps also illustrates the degree of tension and the threat to the sense of the individual self that some twins experience if personal boundaries are not observed. Romulus went on the build the city of Rome and ruled there for many years.

The issues of boundaries and birth right feature in other myths about twins too. With Jacob and Esau, and Horus and Set, the issues of boundaries is so important for the twins that, like Romulus and Remus, they kill or rob each other to preserve them. This links with issues about identity for twins and the intimate bond between them, the bond that is an indelible part of the identity for both twins, but alongside which they have to define a boundary between their individual and their twin identity.

Jacob and **Esau** were born to childless Isaac and Rebekah (Genesis, 25) after Isaac pleaded with the Lord to give him a child. The babies struggled together in her womb and when she questioned the Lord about this, she was told:

> Two nations are in thy womb, and two manner of people shall be separated from thy bowels; and the one people shall be stronger than the other people; and the elder shall serve the younger. And when her days to be delivered were fulfilled, behold, there were twins in her womb. (Genesis, 25:23)

Thus the rivalry between Jacob and Esau started before birth, and as God foretold, would last throughout their lives. Esau was the firstborn, and Jacob was born grasping at the heel (*yaakov*) of his brother, trying to get out first, struggling for power and personal advantage from the beginning.

Jacob and Esau were in a lifelong struggle for power. Jacob was a quiet thoughtful man, but he was scheming and deceitful. In contrast, Esau was impulsive and lacking in thoughtfulness. Jacob took advantage of this to gain power. When Esau arrived back from hunting, he said he felt faint with hunger, and asked Jacob for a bowl of lentils. Jacob gave it to him only on condition that Esau, the firstborn, exchanged his birth right for the food (thus ceding his right to the inheritance of goods and position). Esau reasoned that as he was starving, he would have no further use for his birth right and willingly gave it up to Jacob.

Later, Jacob again used his twin Esau's weakness to his own advantage. When Isaac was dying and wanted to bless his firstborn son, Jacob conspired with his mother to deceive his father into blessing him instead of Esau. Jacob was smooth-skinned while Esau was hairy. To enable the deception Jacob wore a sheepskin on his arms (impersonating Esau) to mislead the nearly blind Isaac into thinking that he was Esau. There are also some suggestions that Isaac knew it was Jacob impersonating Esau, but went along with the deception.

Esau was furious at having been cheated out of his inheritance. In fear, Jacob left home to avoid Esau's wrath at being robbed and went to live in the land of Laban, with his mother's brother. The hatred between Esau and Jacob was such that they lived apart for many years and the descendants of Esau (Edom) were regarded as the persecutors of Jacob's people, the Jews (Israel). Jacob and Esau represented conflicting dimensions of power and authority. Jacob was the intelligent manipulator, who sought power and was to become Israel (literally one who struggles with God), the leader of his tribe. Esau would be deposed by Jacob and become a non-Jewish imperial ruler who was a hunter, a man of the land and animals.

Jacob and Esau were eventually reconciled. The actual meeting was tense but non-violent, which contained tears of both joy at reconciliation and of bitter hatred; a meeting at which the twins demonstrated that they had both matured and could reconcile their differences rather than attempt to destroy each other.

As with Romulus and Remus, the rivalry between these twins when they were young was such that it seemed there was no possibility of resolution of it other than by total separation or the death of one. It was a twinship enmeshed in mutual hatred and enmity. But, like Romulus and Remus, they became nation-builders.

Amphion and **Zethus** in Greek mythology were another twin pair who created a city—Thebes. They were the twin sons of Zeus by Antiope, though Pausanias writes that Zethus was the son of Antiope's husband Epopeus, and Amphion the divine child of Zeus—another example of double paternity. As children, the twins were left to die on Mount Cithaeron but were found and brought up by a shepherd. Amphion became a great singer and musician after Hermes taught him to play and gave him a golden lyre. Zethus was a hunter and herdsman who had a great interest in breeding cattle.

After they had searched for and rejoined their mother, they built and fortified the walls of the city of Thebes. Zethus carried huge blocks of stone while Amphion used the sounds of his magic lyre so the stones moved of their own will and gently slid into place in the walls. Amphion married Niobe. Zethus married Thebe, after whom the city of Thebes was named.

Twin heroes may be same or opposite sex. Where they are opposite sex, they are usually a reproductive pair, and are often the founders of a particular group of people.

Another aspect that mythical twins have represented is that of the social principles of our societies, as illustrated by **Isis, Osiris, Horus, Set, and Nephthys**. Osiris was a primeval king of Egypt in ancient Egyptian mythology, around the twenty-fourth century BCE and he and his twin siblings represent both religious ideas and regional struggles.

Isis, Osiris, Horus, Set, and Nephthys were born to Geb and Nut. The five children were born over a period of five days, at a time when those days were not counted in the calendar. All the children were regarded as brothers and sisters but were essentially quintuplets as they shared the womb. Horus was also variably believed to be either their brother, or the son of Isis and Osiris. It was sometimes thought that Osiris and Isis were so in love they had intercourse in the womb (Raphael-Leff, 1990).

Osiris was known for his gentleness and he embodied the spirit of renewal, of vegetation that dies with the harvest, and is reborn when the grain sprouts. He civilised Egypt and he travelled around the world spreading the benefits of his rule. He married his twin sister Isis, who was also renowned for her good works. When Osiris was abroad, Isis governed judiciously.

In contrast to Osiris's goodness, Set was regarded as the incarnation of the spirit of evil, the personification of the arid desert, of drought and darkness, in eternal opposition to the spirit of good, the fertile earth, life-bringing water, and light in perpetual renewal, represented by Osiris. "All that is creation and blessing comes from Osiris; all that is destruction and perversity arises from Set." (Larousse, 1959, p. 19)

Set hated Osiris's goodness, creativity, and power, and his harmonious marriage to their sister Isis. He was the personification of envious aggression and destructiveness, attacking all good and life-giving processes. "The struggle between the two brothers is the war between the desert and the fertile earth, between the drying wind and vegetation, aridity and fecundity, darkness and light." (ibid., p. 17) So in this pair of twin siblings we again see one representing light, the other darkness, but in an antagonistic rather than a cooperative way.

Set plotted to kill Osiris. Isis knew of Set's plots against Osiris, and she protected Osiris from Set. But one day Set conspired with others to lure Osiris to a banquet and then he fooled him into lying in a richly ornamented carved casket. Set then sealed the casket so that Osiris died. Set threw the casket into the Nile from whence it floated into the sea, and across to Byblos. Isis was distraught, and tore her clothes and cut her hair in mourning. Eventually Isis learned of the location of the casket and she went to reclaim Osiris's body and bury it as had been prescribed. She shed her tears on Osiris's body and hid it in the swamp. But Set found the body and cut it into fourteen pieces, throwing them far and wide. Isis patiently searched and found thirteen of the fragments; the fourteenth, Osiris's phallus, had been eaten by a Nile crab (forever accursed for this crime). Isis used her magical powers to join the pieces together and reconstituted the body of Osiris, but without his penis. She then performed the rights of embalmment (creating the first mummy—Raphael-Leff, 1990), and thus restored the murdered god Osiris to eternal life. Osiris's magical restoration had, however, left him emasculated.

Set had married his twin sister Nephthys and he ruled Egypt in Osiris's absence, creating disorder and division. Nephthys helped Isis find Osiris's body so that Isis could restore him. Horus, the child born to Isis, was magically conceived after Osiris's death and reconstitution, and he later avenged his father. He challenged Set for the throne and restored order to Egypt, counteracting Set's destructive activities.

Osiris, once resurrected and from thenceforward secure from the threat of death, chose not to regain his throne, and he preferred to depart from this earth and retire to the "Elysian Fields". Here he warmly welcomed the souls of the just and reigned over the dead.

Thus these twin siblings represent the social principles of order and disorder, morality, justice, death, and the after-life. Twins in mythology and legend exemplify danger of the processes of deadly aggression and splitting of the self, division amongst of peoples, and the need for a recognition and respect for difference and mature relatedness to others.

Twins are regarded as linked with the weather in many areas of Africa. In Egypt, *Shu* and *Tefnut* are seen as stars shining in the constellation of the heavens. *Shu* is the wind god, *Tefnut* the sender of rain. Amongst the Fon of Dahomey, West Africa, there is a creation myth in which the primeval twins *Mawu*, female (representing the moon and living in the west), came together with *Lisa*, male (representing the sun and living in the east), at the time of an eclipse. Their unity represents the order of the universe. In one legend, they were the children of *Nana Buluku* who created the world. In another, they created the world and were the parents of all the other gods, including the twin gods of storm with their power over thunder and lightning. *Mawu* is the goddess of fertility, joy, and rest. *Lisa* is the god of day, heat, and strength. So we see echoes of the Osiris–Isis myth in these stories.

Cultural practices

Overview

In many countries in the world, a special social significance is attributed to twins, and, as such, twins are often integral to social and cultural systems in the beliefs of those people. This practice goes as far back as prehistoric times, and at a burial site in Thailand there is evidence that newborn twins had been interred in a manner distinct from other infant burials. Excavations in Belgium have revealed Iron Age remains suggestive of the practice of twin murder.

Until we had a sufficient understanding of the processes that lay behind the birth of twins, developed in the last hundred or so years, the arrival of twin babies would have been regarded with fear and awe. To make sense of this troubling occurrence, elaborate legends, religious cults, and ritual ceremonies have been created in relation to twins all over the world. These beliefs and practices vary from the elevation of the twins to god-like status, to the other extreme—horror and the consequent murder of the twins. Both the idealisation with its associated rituals, and the murder relating to twin births are based on the belief that there is something unnatural about twins, and beneficial or malign supernatural powers are attributed to them.

Monozygotic twin births occur at a constant rate of one in 286 all over the world. The figures for dizygotic live twin births range from low rates of one in 150 births in Latin America, South Asia, and South-East Asia, to the highest rates of twinning across Central Africa in Benin, where the national average rates of twin birth are about one in eighteen. In West Africa, the rate amongst the Yoruba in Nigeria is high, one in twenty-five twin births. As I will discuss below, the Yoruba are famous for their customs relating to twins and the small wooden carved statues they make of twins who have died. Different ethnic groups within the same area have different rates of twin birth, suggesting that there are several factors at work including hereditary traits for twin births. Sub-Saharan Africa has the highest infant mortality rate and the differences in rates of twin birth between this region and Asia and Latin America could therefore be even higher. In North America and Europe the intermediate rates of one twin birth in sixty to eighty has changed. Currently in the West, the rates of dizygotic twin birth have increased to one in forty as a result of older maternal age at conception as women tend to delay pregnancy, and of the increasing use of fertility treatment in which more than one embryo is implanted. Fertility treatment also increases the possibilities of embryos splitting because of the hormones used in the treatment.

An exploration of the way different societies perceive twins is reflected in the practices relating to twins, and they may vary at different times in a particular group's own history. The acceptance, rejection, infanticide, and celebratory or cleansing rituals performed to protect the family and society at the birth of twins are linked with the religious beliefs attached to twin birth. Some twins may be killed because they are less viable than other infants, or for population control, but others are killed because they are thought to have been inappropriately conceived and pose a danger to the society. Among some people where resources are especially scarce, like the Bushmen of Southern Africa, the birth of babies is spaced, and twins or any babies born too soon after the last one will also be killed. If the family and tribe can afford to support the birth of two babies, they are more likely to be used as part of a system of belief.

Twins may be regarded as sacred and are often believed to possess extraordinary powers. They are regarded as supernatural and are feared. If allowed to live, they are revered and hold a special place in society. On the other hand they may be considered to be an extreme danger to parents and the society into which they are born. The powers of twins, good or malign, are sometimes extended to their parents. Where the birth of twins is regarded as a cause for celebration, the twins are thought to be gods or the children of gods, and the bringers of good luck and good fortune. However, even if twins are seen as a blessing, special purification ceremonies must be performed to protect them, the parents, and the society from evil. Proper precautions in relation to the birth must strictly observed or the birth of twins may bring ill fortune or ill health upon the family or society. These special performances are designed to reinstate harmony with the upper world of the gods. Some African tribes associate twins with cosmic phenomena such as lightning, thunder, and rain. Twins are often connected with rain, and with the gods of rain and fertility. The powers possessed by twins are generally held to lie in the control of the weather and the promotion of fertility—two linked factors.

But where there is idealisation, the obverse side lurks just below the surface. The dark side of the idealisation is not just the denigration of twins, but the demonisation, the belief that twins are evil, unclean, children of evil spirits or demons, harbingers of bad luck or catastrophe. They are seen as uncanny, equivocal, inauspicious, often expressly ascribed to divine intervention, which is feared. As a result of such fears, in some places not only are twins unwelcome, but one or both may be banished or killed at birth, and often the mother is also killed or exiled as unclean, suspected of having consorted with an evil spirit, or being guilty of adultery. These suspicions allow the society to feel justified in killing one or both twin babies, and sometimes their mother too.

Fortunately, in some societies the custom for twins to be killed or exposed and left to die has been somewhat ameliorated over time, and the twins are allowed to live. But while the penalty for twin birth has been lightened, the twins are still regarded with apprehension or as dangerous, and their birth is accompanied by rituals and ceremonies to ward off evil. Hastings (1921) offers a comprehensive description of practices relating to twins throughout the world.

The stories relating to the conception of twins are based on religious and cultural beliefs linked with the way of life of a particular group, and they have a mythical status. Both twins may be regarded as the children of god, or one of the twins is the child of a god or spirit—sometimes an evil spirit. Thus twins are often believed to be the result of divine intervention or of some form of sexual irregularity (adultery, mother consorting with a god or devil). It is also believed that twins may have been involved in that sexual irregularity (incest—see below).

Amongst some African tribes, twins and the mother are killed immediately and cleansing rituals are performed. The brutality of some of these killings and rituals is an indication of the level of fear that the birth of twins arouses in the people concerned. In some, the female or weaker twin is killed. Amongst some of the Ambo Bantu tribes, royal twins are killed but those of commoners are allowed to survive. Conversely, the Balinese treat royal twins well, but kill those of commoners. The ways in which twins are seen will depend on the particular religious beliefs of the people concerned and a cultural diffusion of concepts and ideas.

Amongst the Nilotic and Bantu tribes, there are different twin cults with varying perceptions of twin babies. Many tribes see twins as a token of fertility for the cattle and crops, bringers of rain and wind. Until recent times, there was no distinction made between monozygotic and dizygotic twins—an interesting observation in view of the powerful twinning processes between twins, regardless of their zygosity. Amongst some tribes, same sex twins were referred to only as brother or sister, whereas opposite sex twins were called twins. Sometimes opposite sex twins are preferred to same sex twins. There are widespread customs in giving the twins special names and making sure to always treat them alike. The functions attributed to the first- and second-born twins may vary. The older twin may be considered a hero, and the second a healer.

The beliefs about twins and the consequent practices are worldwide and have been observed in Africa, Asia, the Far East, North and South America, Australia, ancient Europe, and even England. I will look at some of the better-known practices and the associated beliefs, and also some of the painful examples of slaughter based again on religious beliefs. If we consider the intensity of reactions to the birth of twins, either the joy and celebration of something extraordinarily special, or on the other hand the dread and horror with which they are greeted and the appalling cruelty inflicted on the twins and the mother, we must assume that twins represent much more than just the birth of two babies when only one was expected. Twin births are not at all uncommon in many areas where these practices are carried out, so there is nothing innately strange or abnormal about them and other factors account for they way they are treated.

Some newborn twins are seen as fetish children (inhabited by a spirit). One twin may be regarded as a "ghost" twin, imbued with the spirit of a god or a demon. Sometimes the "ghost" twin is killed. If it is believed that the mother of the twins is unclean and will defile anything she touches, she may not drink from the same spring as others in the community, and often will die of thirst and hunger, or kill herself. Where this sentence is mitigated, the mother may be exiled to a "twin town" with her babies, either forever or for a period of time until she is considered to have been cleansed. The people who perform the killing of the twins may be professionals (for example a slave dedicated to this function), or it may be the grandmother or father who kills one or both twins, by smothering or exposing them. They may be left out in the bush to perish, placed in a pot or a sack hanging from a tree to die, buried alive, or even burnt.

In other cultures twins are regarded as having a personal connection with particular apes, birds, or a crocodile. Among various tribes of the north-west coast of North America, twins are linked with grizzly bears and other land animals, or to salmon or other fish. The twins are believed to be a reincarnation of such creatures rather than directly generated by them within the mother. The twins are seen as grizzly bears in human form and, when a twin dies, his soul goes back to the grizzly bears and he becomes one of them.

When twins are born, the twins and their parents are, as a rule, secluded from interaction with the world until various ceremonies are completed. Occasionally a twin birth is seen as a joy and frankly welcomed, as in the Herero of Namibia, and in the nomadic Masai of Kenya. Rituals to celebrate the birth of twins or to cleanse them and the family of evil that might ensue, may include the drinking of palm wine, hanging cowrie shells on the twins or the mother, or rituals where the parents or mother are quarantined to the house for a period of time, or have to walk round the house in a particular direction. They may not be allowed to enter or exit the house via the door, but only through a gap that has been created at the back of the hut. When a twin dies at birth or later, it is common to find that mourning is prohibited and that particular death rituals must be performed.

Amongst some communities, the birth of twins of different sexes is regarded as a serious situation, as they are thought to have had an incestuous relationship in utero, because they have shared the womb. It is held that their connection in the womb has been too close: it has been sinful, amounting to prenatal incest. The idea of prenatal incest is not always frowned upon in opposite sex twins. Among the highest castes of Balinese, opposite sex twins are seen as "betrothed". This may have its origin from a time when there were no taboos against brother–sister incest, and when such twins at marriageable age used to be made to marry one another. It may also link with ancient Egyptian practices where royal brothers and sisters married. In ancient Assyria and Babylonia, opposite sex twins of lower-class birth were regarded as a bad omen, foreshadowing the death of the king. However, amongst royal families twin marriage was permissible. The Mohave of Southern California believe that opposite sex twins have been married in a former life in heaven.

Thus amongst many people, twins may be seen as the result of divine impregnation, or impregnation by two fathers and hence adultery by the mother, of superfetation (the occurrence of a second conception during pregnancy, giving rise to embryos of different ages in the uterus), or as a ghost of the dead. It may be thought that mother has trespassed on the sacred place of a ghost whose power resides there, and who has impregnated her. If the second child is seen as a result of the mother's infidelity, and if the father had any suspicion as to his wife's loyalty, the father would have the right of deciding upon the birth of a child whether it should be brought up or destroyed, and the child was often killed. Thus it was felt to be excusable to expose or put to death twins and triplets.

A number of mediaeval legends among the Germans and other Teutonic peoples are elaborations of this theme. In mediaeval Europe it was believed that twins were born because mother had been unfaithful to her husband. In Scotland, it was believed that water from the well of St Mungo would ensure a twin birth, or that infertility would follow a twin birth. In Sussex, it was thought that if one twin died, the other would be left with healing powers. In Wales, as recently as the twentieth century, twins were associated with good luck and fertile influences. In Bulgaria, the mothers of the bride and groom would simultaneously drink brandy to prevent the birth of twin grandchildren. In Eastern Europe, the Huzuls of the Carpathian Mountains believed that the birth of twins indicated that the parents would die early. The idea of the eating of double fruits or nuts (joined together on a single stalk) has also been held to account for the birth of twins. In ancient England, around Malvern, it was said that the quantity of nuts produced is a presage of the number of children to be born in the year, and double nuts presage a considerable number of twins.

In Japan, twins were regarded with distaste and the twin birth was concealed. If both twins were males, one might be given away to be reared by a trusted courtier as his own child. But the child given away would retain his birth right, and if the other twin died, he would be secretly returned to the parents. In the nineteenth and earlier centuries, the mother was treated with pity and aversion. There were disputes about which twin would be given away, according to which was considered the eldest—which was born first, or which was apparently conceived first as the guest and therefore born second. The theory was that the maternal and paternal essences met to produce a child. When there was an excess of essence, twins were conceived, one strong and healthy, the other weak, depending on the potency of the extra essences. The weaker child was considered to be the host in utero and the other the guest, implying that the healthier baby will be kept by the parents, as guests have an honoured social position in Japanese society. The mother was considered to be particularly prone to shock at the birth of twins and had to be prepared carefully for her encounter with them. Little is recorded of female twins, either because they were weeded out as not worthy of life, or simply not considered worth mentioning.

North and South American Indians

The cultural practices amongst the North and South American Indians are based on mythical beliefs, which I will briefly describe. In many groups of Native Americans, myths about divine twins are linked with magical powers. The divine twins battle to create social principles, often exacted through their intense rivalry. In this function, they are central to the development of community. Common themes about twins in these cultures are the intense closeness of twins, the idea of shared souls, and a desperate longing to be reunited after parting.

Several pairs of mythical twins are described on the Western American continent. Of these the best known are the twins Ioskeha and Tawiscara of Iroquoian tradition, among the Five Nations tribes in New York State. According to their legend, a woman named Ataensic fell down through a rift in the sky upon the primeval waters, for there was as yet no land. On the advice of the turtle, the animals dived, brought up soil, put it on the turtle's back, and so formed the earth to receive the falling heroine, who was pregnant and promptly gave birth to a daughter. The daughter became pregnant in her turn with two boys, Ioskeha and Tawiscara. The latter was evil by nature: he refused to be born in the natural manner and broke his way out through his mother's side or armpit, ending her life with his own birth. As the brothers grew up, Ioskeha went about providing the earth with water, which until that time had been arid. But Tawiscara, the evil twin, attempted to foil him by creating a gigantic frog to swallow all the water.

A quarrel ensued, as in the case of Romulus and Remus. Ioskeha used the horns of a deer and vanquished Tawiscara, whose weapon was only a branch of the wild rose, and Ioskeha drove Tawiscara away to the extreme west. Tawiscara's blood gushed from him at every step and turned into flint as it fell. The victor then established his lodge in the Far East, opened a cave in the earth, and brought forth all kinds of land animals, and he created men. He instructed them in the art of making fire and in the growing of maize. He brought fertility to the soil. Ioskeha, like Osiris, is therefore the culture hero and divine helper of the Huron-Iroquois. The birth, deeds, rivalry, and combat of these heavenly twins are the foundation of their beliefs. We see here again how the development of social principles amongst the community is reflected in the temperaments and actions attributed to the twin brothers. Mythical twins are used to explain unconscious but potent forces internal to individuals and to the community itself in its business of nation building.

Amongst other groups of North American Indians, the Navaho of Arizona and the Zuni of New Mexico believe in a myth of divine twins fathered by the sun (like the Asvins). The twins work to reduce the dangerous forces that threaten mankind, and they instruct men in the art of survival. Both the Navajo and the Apaches called the twins Killer-of-enemy-gods and Child-of-the-waters. The enemy-gods are the monsters that inhabited the primordial earth, and were exterminated by the twins to make it habitable for mankind. The South American Indians also believe in a pair of divine twins who bring with them the gifts of fire and the arts.

Amongst some North and South American Indians, it was the custom to kill one or both twins and sometimes to kill the mother in a ritualistic manner. The twins might be buried alive alongside the mother. Some tribes killed the female of opposite sex twins. The Californian Indians used to kill all twins, whereas the Yuman Indians of the Colorado River link twins with a divine presence, and believe that twins have come down from heaven to assist in agriculture because they are linked with rain-making—a common belief found amongst some African tribes too. Twins are often associated either positively or negatively with rain and drought.

The Yuman dress twins alike in red, white, and black, the colours of the clouds. They believe the twins have to be encouraged to remain on the earth and offer them special gifts and privileges, and it is only when they have married that the twins will become firmly attached to the earth. They are thought to be clairvoyants and they possess special powers.

The Mohave apply special face paint to female twins. They believe that twins lived in heaven prior to their descent to earth. There are more twins in heaven than come down to earth, and they may visit earth as sightseers. Twins always visit earth in human form so as to experience human life. They do not have a mother and father in heaven and were not created by anything supernatural. The earthly parents of the twins contribute to the bodies of twins, as they do to other babies, but they are not held responsible for creating the souls of the twins. Twins' souls differ from those of normal human beings in that they are immortal, though they may lose their immortality in certain conditions. If a drought is likely, the heavenly group of twins will roll rocks around to cause thunder, and therefore rain. In heaven the twins drink rainwater, but on earth they do what other humans do and drink pump water.

Mohave twins are believed to select their mother from amongst the pregnant women, before the unborn baby has an identity of its own, before the sixth month of pregnancy. Where twins are prevalent in certain lineages, it is assumed that previously incarnated twins were satisfied with their treatment by that family, so more will encounter a good reception. They descend to earth via lightning, thunder, and rain.

There is a general belief that the firstborn twin is the younger one, as the Yuma usually allow the younger children to walk ahead in order to keep an eye on them. No special privileges are offered to the firstborn twin. Same sex twins are assumed to have been siblings in heaven, opposite sex twins have been married in heaven, and there is a profound affinity between the souls of the twins. Opposite sex twins do not marry each other on earth, and do not display any jealousy towards the spouse of their twin. If one twin dislikes the earth, he will make himself ill and die, so as to return to heaven. The other twin will follow because he longs to be reunited with his twin. No twins become incarnated twice, and they do not really die—they go back to heaven. Overall the birth of twins is considered to be an undisguised blessing. When they die they are cremated, as are other people, since they possess a human body, while their souls return to heaven.

A different line of belief amongst the Mohave holds that twins are people who have died and come back to earth. These contradictory beliefs may be the result of ambivalence about twins amongst some groups, linked with sibling rivalry and elaborate stories to cover it up in the interests of the preservation of the tribe.

Other groups

In India there are specific bereavement customs that are followed in twin deaths. The spiritual connection between twins is thought to be too close and rites are performed to break the closeness. If one twin dies, it is believed that the other will too. It is feared that the dead twin may be a danger to the living twin and steps must be taken to separate them. Various effigies of dead twins may be kept and looked after.

The ancient Peruvians held that one of the twins was the son of the lightning, to which they prayed as the lord and creator of rain. The earthly parents were made to undergo various taboos and ceremonies. Amongst some groups twins may be considered to have a double spirit.

The treatment of the birth of twins in various different cultural situations throughout the world offers a fascinating insight into our perceptions of twins and what they represent for the different communities. It is interesting that the same phenomenon, the birth of twins, can stir such diametrically opposed actions in relation to the twins. It is evident that twins arouse something deep and primitive within us, something that may seem to threaten our sense of being and continuity, particularly our sense of having a unique identity, and threatens the community.

As already noted, the twin birth rate amongst black Africans is higher than that in Europe, by as much as twice among some tribal groups. There are some theories that suggest the excitement and the ritual treatment of twins is based on their scarcity. However, the actual birth rates of twins indicate that this theory does not stand up to scrutiny. Based on these statistics, neither would the notion of twins being seen as an abnormality, although they are sometimes linked with animals that give birth to more than one infant. Twins are sometimes regarded as having a "psychic unity", a situation to be revered or abhorred, the twins to be deified or separated, though ritual or death.

The differences of practice in relation to twins in various cultures must originate from both internal and external factors. I have already explored internal factors. I will now look at external factors and their impact on cultural practice, and how they may have been propagated. Outside influences may be both vertical and horizontal, both contemporary and ancient. The learning from other older cultures would be passed down from one generation to another and also between and amongst the various communities. In a number of cultures, it is apparent that the rituals and customs to deal with the birth of twins are likely to be based on religious beliefs linked with a sun cult, similar to that evolved in ancient Egypt.

It is likely that ancient Egyptian practices and beliefs would have spread to other African groups. Jeffreys (1963) traces the transmission of a sun god culture from Ancient Egypt, originating in the Fertile Crescent of the Nile valley, to other parts of Africa (and Europe and Asia), as a result of migration up and down Africa at various times. Cultures borrowed from each other creating hybrid cultures. The divine kings of Egypt were considered to be "children of the sun", and the customs they followed have been found amongst the Yoruba, Jukun, Ibo, and Baganda tribes in Africa. The sky gods are linked with the human spirit, and rain is associated with the rain god, Tefnut, and with twins. However, the emphasis on the transmission of Egyptian belief systems is not held universally, and the similarity in practices may be the result of independent development from a common basis in an ancient Hamitic culture.

In all the cultures following a sun god, twins are presented to the king or god, indicating that he owns them. Twins are given special stereotyped names depending on which twin was born first, or gender. In Egypt, as in contemporary African tribes one twin may be regarded as a ghost or spirit being. In some African tribes, twins are kept and rituals performed to protect them and the parents and community; in others twins are destroyed at birth, or one twin is killed—the one judged to be the "ghost" child. As with the myth of Castor and Pollux, one twin is thought to be mortal, the other one linked to a god or spirit, or in some cases an evil spirit. Among the ancient Egyptians, and in contemporary African tribes, twins are considered to share a soul, or be one pair in two bodies.

In some groups in Africa, except the Nguni (amongst the Bantu groupings), it is customary and considered justifiable to kill one or both twins because they are regarded as evil omens who must be got rid of before they bring disaster on their parents and families. Amongst the Shangana-Tonga, Venda, Tswana, and Transvaal Sotho, twins are killed and must be buried in the moist soil of river banks or in the shade of a hut where they will be cooled and prevented from burning up the land. They are considered to be ritually impure and their bodies to be hot, driving the rain away.

The Zulus of Southern Africa regard twins as unlucky and either the grandmother will suffocate the second child, or the father will place a lump of earth in the child's mouth in order to protect himself from losing strength. Twins that survive are regarded as strong and brave in war and lead others into battle. The death of a twin is not mourned, as that would offend the communal ancestral spirit, *amatonga*. Twins are regarded as being of one flesh, and there are many beliefs linking them with the supernatural.

The Igbo (also known as Ibo) of southeast Nigeria are followers of a sun cult, but they destroy twins at birth because they believe there has been an unholy alliance during sleep with an evil spirit that results in a second child being born. The second child is thought to house the spirit of an animal. This idea is linked with that of the ancient Egyptian "ghost child", but the spirit concerned is believed to be a malevolent one, not a god.

Thus, amongst many peoples, twins are regarded as sacred—a state of being that may be a source of peril, or it may be a source of blessing. There is always some ambivalence about the sacred, and depending on the particular beliefs of a community, twins will be treated as a blessing, as god or gifts of the gods, or as a danger to the family and society, and rituals will be performed to protect society.

I will describe some of the twin-related customs and beliefs in a little more detail amongst three different African tribes.

The Yoruba of southwestern Nigeria

The Yoruba people have amongst the highest birth rate for DZ twins in the world, probably as a result of hereditary factors, though there has been a suggestion that the particular diet common in this group may also be a contributing factor. As twins suffer a higher risk of mortality than do single born children, the consequence of the high rate of twin births is that there is greater infant mortality. In order to cope with the high rate of infant mortality, the Yoruba people have developed a "twin belief system". This enables them to deal with the deaths of their twins and mourn their loss, and the loss to the society as a whole.

The Yoruba believe in immortality and reincarnation of the soul. In the Yoruba religion, the supreme deity is *Olodumare* who is supported by secondary gods. Everyone on earth has an ancestral guardian spirit or a soul counterpart in the sky that duplicates their ancestors. The soul is cyclically reborn. Twins share a double soul and the spirit double has been born on earth. Sometimes there is confusion about which is a divine being and which mortal, so they are both treated as sacred.

As late as the seventeenth century, ritual killing of a mother of twins and one or both twins was common practice amongst the Yoruba. Alternatively, the mother and babies might be banished either temporarily or permanently, to twin towns. She might be allowed to return with one twin, or with neither. The belief was that the birth of two babies indicated that two fathers were involved in the pregnancy, thus indicating adultery by the mother, either with an evil spirit or another man. She had thus been "defiled". There was concern that a paternity suit would ensue and that this would disturb the community. Also the social structure would be threatened if two people of the same age were admitted, in a community where seniority mattered.

At that time, the newborn twins were ritually sacrificed, as they were feared as the embodiment of ill omens. They were regarded as changelings, *abiku*, destined to die. However, this practice of twin infanticide changed, and twins are now revered and protected—again we see the two sides of the coin, idealisation versus death. The Yoruba have created a myth to deal with this change of practice in relation to twins.

The idea that twins are changelings originates in the story about the farmer who was angry that the colobus monkeys kept raiding his fields, stealing his produce. He set about chasing them away, then killing them in the fields and wood. But they kept returning. Meanwhile his wife became pregnant but the baby died at birth. This happened several times, and at last the farmer sought the advice of a seer, who told him that as long as he hunted and killed the monkeys, his wife would have stillborn babies. The unborn babies were changelings, babies substituted by the monkeys. The souls of the changelings were to return to the monkeys after birth so the babies died, and this would continue until the father allowed the monkeys to feed on his crops. Experiencing the repeated trauma of stillborn infants, the farmer relented and allowed the monkeys onto his land. The farmer's wife then gave birth to normal twins, the first in the land, who survived.

Twins were given the protection of the King, and now twins are the cause of celebration, as the family and society rejoice in their birth. They are perceived as bestowing happiness, health, and prosperity on the family if they are properly cared for. The mother of the twins has to dance and sing in the marketplace with the twins to the beat of a drum. She will be paid for doing so and she is to request alms. Thus she will become wealthy. But twins are also capable of sowing disaster, disease, and death, and are therefore treated with respect, love, and great care to avert this. Their upbringing is more permissive than that of other children.

Twins are regarded as having unstable temperaments and are placated by giving them the best food, clothes, and jewellery. They are linked with the god of thunder and lightning, *Shango*, who is also the provider of material wealth. Thus they are *Thunderchildren*. They are also linked with *Oko Sheji*, the "husband of the twins". Twins are regarded as living in three different worlds at the same time—the bush (forests and uncultivated land where wild animals and spirits dwell), the spirit world, and the human world. They bridge the gap between the world of the gods and world of humans.

The firstborn of the twins is always called *Taiwo*, which means having the first taste of the world. The second twin, called *Kehinde*, which means "arriving after the other", is the senior twin and sends his junior partner out into the world to see what it is like before venturing out himself. When *Taiwo* cries, it is a signal for *Kehinde* to come out. *Kehinde* is viewed as more careful, intelligent, and reflective in nature than is *Taiwo*, while *Taiwo* is more curious, adventurous, and relaxed.

Three days after their birth, the parents consult a priest about the twins. The priest drives out the evil spirits that threaten newborn babies. If the priest decides that one twin is possessed by evil spirits that cannot be exorcised, the priest may tell the mother to starve that twin to death. So even in these very early days, the twins are subject to the projections of others declaring one "good", the other "evil". The twins cleared of evil spirits are dedicated to the god of twins, *Orisha Obeiji*. The priest advises the mother on how to treat the twins, what colours they should wear, and what they should eat.

After the birth of twins, the status of the mother is increased and she is envied by the community. Her marital status may be enhanced, especially where there is polygamy and she becomes the favoured wife who has presented her husband with two babies at once. This will enhance the status of the husband whose wealth is judged by the number of children he produces.

Twins share the same combined soul, so if one twin dies, the other will be in mortal danger because the soul has become seriously disturbed, and the balance between the spirit world and human world has been upset. In this event, the family undertakes a special ritual. The priest commissions an artisan to carve a small wooden figure that will be a symbolic substitute for the soul of the dead twin. If both twins die, there will be two statues. The wooden figures are known as *Ere ibeji—ere* means sacred image, *ibi* means born, and *eji* means two. So the phrase means "sacred twin birth". The *Ere* figure is carved in the same sex as the dead twin, but in adult form. It bears a likeness to the twin and will also have kinship scars.

The priest performs the ritual of transferring the soul of the dead twin to the *ibeji*, which becomes a symbolic substitute and dwelling place for the soul of the dead twin. As the immortal soul of the twin is hosted by the *ibeji*, the dead twin is considered as powerful as the living twin and will be cared for by the parents, and later the surviving twin. *Ibejis* are symbolically washed, fed, and clothed. The family do not talk about the twin having died, but rather having "gone travelling", "gone to market", or "gone to Lagos". The *ibeji* are regularly fed with beans and red palm oil, sacred food. They are rubbed with the camwood powder to consecrate them to *Shango*, and they may be painted with indigo and decorated with cowrie shells (symbolising currency).

So what we see is a ritualised grieving process. The twin cult is one of the earliest religious belief systems, dealing with universal superstitions and generating specific customs.

Yoruba beliefs and customs have been observed far afield, among the Yoruba people who were transported to other countries as slaves. The Afro-Cubans think of the Spanish names of Catholic saints as translations of Yoruba names of Orishas into Spanish. Thus Christian twin saints, St Comas and St Damien, are considered to be *ibeji* and are cared for as if they were small children. Similarly, in Brazil, the rituals associated with *ibeji* have been amalgamated with the ceremonies celebrating the twin saints Cosme and Damiao, in a Yorubanisation of Portuguese Brazilian ritual practice.

Yoruban twins occupy an ambivalent position where they were previously demonised, then idealised but regarded as still dangerous, so that rituals must be performed to protect them, their parents, and the society in which they live.

The idea of a shared soul and personality in twins is common to other cultures as well.

The Nuer people of South Sudan

The Nuer of South Sudan believe that the birth of twins poses a grave danger to the family and kin and they take various measures to protect themselves, including arm and leg jewellery, and animal sacrifice. The sacrifice is called "going out to meet the twins". Twins have a special spirit called *Kwoth cuckni* (spirit of twins), which must be respected by sacrifices when they are born. Various taboos prevent them from socialising until after sacrifices have been made to protect them from the danger. The parents of the twins are assumed to be in particular danger from the twins. They are safer if the twins are of opposite sexes. In this case, the boy twin says to his twin sister, "let's kill our mother", and she will counter this by saying "no, who will then dance my wedding dance?" Likewise, when the girl says, "let's kill our father", he will refuse by saying "no, who will then give me a hunting spear and fishing spear?" So neither parent will be killed. However, with same sex twins, the girls will threaten to kill their father and the boys their mother.

Twins must go through a fictional marriage with a person of the opposite sex shortly after they reach puberty, before a twin can marry. Various dances and ceremonies are performed so that they can be properly married later and have sexual relationships. There are also rituals carried out to ensure that both older and younger twins remain fertile. Twin relationships are recognised as being closer than any others. The children and other descendants of twins are therefore regarded as closer than any other family members.

Twins are seen as one person and are regarded as having a single personality. The word they use is *ran* which means "person", without reference to gender, age, or distinguishing features. So their single social personality is something over and above their physical duality, though they are treated as two distinct individuals in ordinary social life. The unity of twins is expressed in certain rituals and symbolically, particularly in relation to ceremonies around marriage and death when the personality changes. When the senior of two male twins marries, the junior twin performs the marriage rituals together with him. Female twins are married on the same day. Where one twin dies, burial ceremonies for the dead twin are not performed because one twin cannot be cut off from the living without the other, thus echoing some of the Yoruba customs. The soul of the dead twin is presumed to live on in the live twin.

When the second twin dies, burial ceremonies are still not performed because twins are considered to be a person of the sky, a *ran nhial*, or a *gat kwoth*, a child of God. The Nuer differ from other peoples that regard twins as godlike in that they believe that twins are birds. A twin may be given a proper name *Dit* meaning bird, or *Gwong*, guineafowl, or *Ngec*, francolin, all being earthbound birds. The Nuer consider it shameful to eat birds or the eggs of birds. For a twin to eat a bird would be a grave sin because birds are also twins and must be respected.

When a twin infant dies, it is said it has "flown away", using a term to denote the flight of birds, *ce par*. Infant twins who die are not buried, but are placed in a reed basket in the fork of a tree, a place where birds rest. Likewise, adult twins are not buried like other people because they are considered to be birds whose souls will fly into the air. Instead their bodies are placed on a hide on top of a platform that has been erected in the grave, and then covered with a second hide. Earth is then carefully patted in place on top of the second hide. This is supposed to protect the bodies from predators who might eat the body and then drink from a pool, so contaminating the water the people drink from.

The idea the twins are birds (rather than just like birds) is closely connected with the Nuer religion. A twin is a special creature, a person of "the above", because of the manner of his conception, and as a special creature, he is a manifestation of spirit. When he dies, his soul flies into the air where things associated with spirit belong. Birds likewise belong to the above. It is not clear whether a twin is said to be a person of the above because he is a bird, or whether he is said to be a bird because he is a person of above. They are both considered to be children of God who belong in the air, birds because they fly, twins because of their conception and birth. A twin birth is a special revelation of the spirit.

The Nuer treat twins as people in everyday life despite the fact that they regard the personality and the soul of twins as birds. They see the relationship as a triadic one between the twins, birds, and God. If one twin dies, the child born after him takes the place of the dead twin, in ceremonies twins have to perform, and he has to respect birds as if he were a twin himself. The ceremonies are performed for the benefit of the living twin, ceremonies that require two people to perform them.

Again, amongst the Nuer, we find that twins are considered to be close to or connected with the gods, and to share a soul, to be one person.

The Bomvana of Pondoland

The Bomvana rejoice in the birth of twins. They believe that God, *uTixo*, the first man, came out of the sea sending forth children and twins. When twins are born, the father goes to the forest and digs up two small euphorbia trees, placing white beads in the place where the euphorbias were. He plants the euphorbias in the hut, next to the mother. The twin babies are ritually washed in a tincture of ground euphorbia root in water. The placentas are buried next to a euphorbia tree and the euphorbias are fenced with thorn bushes to protect them. The ancestral spirits are appeased with the ritual killing of an animal.

The euphorbias must be protected so as not to endanger the life of the twins. Each twin has its own tree and it is believed that if one twin dies, the tree will fade and die. The trees are regarded as protectors of the twins in illness.

Twin boys are circumcised together. Where the twins are opposite sexes, the girl accompanies her twin brother to the ceremony and will sit next to her brother. The person performing the circumcision will pretend to circumcise her but will pass on to her brother, at which time she will leave. Both have their heads shaved and they exchange necklaces. The girl may not have any sexual relationships until her twin brother has healed after the circumcision. So they share the circumcision symbolically, as if they are one.

When one twin dies, the surviving twin exchanges her beads or blanket with those of the dead twin. When the grave has been dug, the surviving twin gets into the grave and lies there for a short time, in the posture of a corpse, and then gets out. There is no weeping and the sign of mourning is the shaven heads of the family. Similarly to Yoruba custom, the dead twin is not regarded as dead, but referred to as "pretending", or "broken off" (like the branch of a tree). If a twin dies as a child, he will be buried next to the euphorbia tree and the surviving child will be washed daily beside the euphorbia trees.

Unlike twins in other tribes, these twins are not regarded as having any powers over rain, but they are able to drive away hail. The child born after the twins, the *imfusi*, is considered to be an additional twin, "the great twin", and to have great potentialities and be subjected to the same rituals.

Cultural belief and mourning practices

As we have seen above, cultural beliefs about twins are reflected the nature of their mourning practices in many civilisations. There are common themes that influence these practices such as the apparent fragility and capriciousness of twins and their need for special treatment; the belief that twins share a soul; and that the death of one twin will be followed by death of the other, as they cannot bear to be parted.

The burial practices vary. In Cameroon, the Bangolan bury twins like a king (*Fon*), on a throne. In East Africa, the Azande bury twins at the roadside. Passers-by will throw a leaf, twig, or grass to protect them from bad luck. The Nsó of West Africa perform ritual sacrifices when twins die. Among the Wanyoro of East Africa there is a long mourning period during which twins are left in a miniature hut.

It is extraordinary how elaborate the stories and rituals are relating to twin birth. It is evident that detailed belief systems have been created to explain the considerable unease that twins arouse, and to attempt to still that unease and avert the danger twins are reputed to pose to the members of the community. While in some communities twins are frankly welcomed, they still have a special status. Even in communities where twin birth is a rather ordinary event, as amongst the Yoruba, the excitement and anxiety is such that action is taken to preserve the sense of cohesion in the community. One would have to conclude that twins represent something very powerful in our unconscious world, something that in a primitive state of mind leads to a perception of twins in which they come to be either idealised or demonised.

The fact that so many creation myths centre around twins is again a pointer to their importance in understanding ourselves. It indicates that we see our psychological birth emerging from a state of twinship, from the early narcissistic twinning with mother, the phantasy twin.

CHAPTER SIX

Twins and doubles in literature

Twins may be used as split-off aspects of self, as doubles, and this double frequently represents the unconscious "dark side" that emerges in a split-off and disowned "evil" character.

When I started research into how twins were used as characters in literature, I was surprised to see how very frequently this happens. No doubt this in part reflects the increasing frequency of actual twins in the world in general. It also indicates our growing understanding of the nature and complexity of twin relationships, and how they can be used to explore issues of personal identity and uniqueness. But twins in literature serve other purposes as well, as I will attempt to unravel. Many books about twins use the stereotyped view of twins as two halves of a whole, or as bound together forever as a psychic unity. They employ the uncanniness of the double to create excitement and intrigue.

Our current preoccupations with identity and a sense of integrity of the self are major preoccupations and are reflected in the use of twins in literature. But the preoccupation is also seen in earlier times. The concept of a double was a feature of Romanticism in the nineteenth and early twentieth century literature, and much of this writing illustrated fears about the threat to the integrity of the self and the dangers posed by splitting or fragmentation of the self. Shakespeare wrote about

twins in the seventeenth century, with an emphasis on mistaken identity and the deep sense of connectedness between twins. Even earlier,
the Bible featured twins, as do other ancient birth and creation myths
and legends.

As I have already written, our fascination with twins originates in
part in our own feelings about ourselves in relation to others, in our
sense of identity with all its uncertainties and doubts. The creation of
a sense of self within the complex set of relationships of parents and
siblings, especially in the early days to mother, raises questions for us
all about who we are. Our identities, deriving from both genetic factors and early relationships, are forged throughout our continuing
development through life and are never complete, though our "signa-
ture", the way in which we and others recognise ourselves, is unique
and identifiable to each of us. But we never seem to feel quite secure in
who we are—it is as if something is missing, perhaps a manifestation of
the longed-for twin!

This unease with ourselves arises in part from our complex mental,
emotional, and psychological make-up, in which we have to manage
and integrate several layers of relatively known and unknown parts
of ourselves. The unconscious aspects of our minds are crucial to our
sense of who we are, even though we only get to know about them
when something unexpected erupts into our conscious world, or in
coded form in our dreams, and in unexpected symptoms that seem
to arise from nowhere. It is not too surprising, therefore, that so many
authors employ what are often regarded as divided characters of twins
and doubles to express and explore aspects of life.

I have spent many hours reading just a moderate selection of
the multitude of published books with twins as central characters,
or even secondary characters. I will explore below how and why
so many authors use this device, and what can we learn about ourselves from the use of twins in what we read? How does a given
book affect the reader? What does the reader feel and identify with?
And what does it tell us about the authors and their motivation for
creating twin characters? What does it represent for them? For some
authors, there is a persistent theme in their work centred around
twins and twinning.

Books about twins cover diverse plots and themes. While I agree
with Juliana de Nooy about the many uses to which twins are put in

the arts, I do believe our fascination with twins lies at the heart of it. As she says:

> ... there is seemingly no limit to the cultural purposes to which twins can be put. Pressed into the service of the imagination, twins can be used to signify not only the unconscious, the divided self, narcissistic love, death, and fear of sexuality, but also the nation, the couple, fertility, eroticism, chance, life choices, uncertain paternity, writing, reality versus image, monstrosity, race relations, sexual difference, indeed any kind of difference, any figure of the Other (another ethnicity, gender class, sexuality) and any duality, and to explore nature-nurture debates in any field.
>
> Stories of twins are remarkable not only for their number and frequency, but for their diversity. Identical, non-identical, conjoined, mutant, telepathic, homicidal, buddies, tricksters, soulmates, long-lost siblings or jealous rivals, twins populate stories that may share very little in terms of plot, character, genre or audience. (de Nooy, 2005, p. 4)

While twins may be depicted as physically different, boy or girl, same sex but different or alike, the internal and eternal twin bond is central to the tension that is played out in twin stories. Reflecting what may occur in real life, separations between the twins may be unbearably painful, and create a sense of longing that only ceases when the twins are joyfully reunited. For many fictional twins, the death of one twin leaves the other not only painfully bereft, but frequently close to death themselves, as if one cannot survive without the other. For actual twins, of course, the bereavement will be intense and sometimes lifelong, but seldom heralds the death of the surviving twin. It may feel to the surviving twin that they too will die soon, as has been illustrated in case material and the written accounts of survivors. The surviving twin feels a part of herself has died, as is common in any bereavement, but the fear of death may be much greater in twins because of their intense unconscious sensate bond.

Fictional twins may be used to represent different aspects of a character, as a concrete expression of a known or a knowable part, or a hidden darker side. They may represent desired alternative aspects of the self, or discarded aspects. In our concerns with identity and the fragmented nature of the self, we use twins to explore who we are or wish to be. Very many of the twins in novels are monozygotic and apparently identical in appearance. They give voice to our ubiquitous longing for a perfect soulmate, an alter ego with a special and profound closeness to oneself—the idealised twin of infancy.

The earliest stories about twins are myths—creation myths about the beginnings of the world, about the creation of nations. These stories are complex and subtle, and often feature both the intimate bonding between twins, and the intense, sometimes murderous, rivalry between them. I have written about these in Chapter Five.

From Shakespeare onwards, the twin relationship has often been used in literature to exploit the comic potential of mistaken identity. This also has important implications, such as in the courts of law where mistaken identity can have very serious consequences. In all kinds of literature, from children's stories of cute twin children up to pranks and devilment, through both serious and less serious books, and great literary works, the dichotomies of the twin relationship are used to explore the intrinsic duality in human nature, common to us all. This duality arises from internal conflicts we all experience and try to manage. The ways in which we view ourselves change over time and in different situations, though a central core remains and is strengthened as we resolve our internal conflict. However, the central core may be disturbed by powerful or traumatic events.

With fictional twins, the issues of mistaken identity and interchangeability play with our real-life insecurities about ourselves. Where there is confusion between two people, as there is sometimes between actual twins, the central core of the self seems to be threatened. We depend on both internal factors and external recognition for a more secure sense of ourselves both in relation to others and to our own internal state of mind. It is as if we have a porous membrane around us so that experiences will create links that travel both inwards and outwards in relation to others and to events in our lives. Each event will to a greater or lesser degree affect our sense of ourselves at a particular moment in time and space, our sense of wellbeing, of comfort or discomfort in our own skins.

For twins, the profound relationship with the other twin is to greater or lesser degrees part of the sense of identity of each of them in their own particular way. As a result, the membrane holding the sense of self or identity is more complex for twins. We could imagine it as a thick membrane surrounding the twins in their twinship, and a thinner personal membrane between them. So they are closer to each other, and more distant from and less affected by, other people. Where there have been developmental difficulties, it is as if the external and internal membranes are too porous and they will experience frequent fluctuations in their sensitivity and sense of identity, in relation to the external world.

Thus, we are constantly in a state of flux about who we are at a particular moment and some of the ways this is reflected in the literature are through the device of both doubles and twins. In stories, as in real life, twins may use the twinship to bolster their sense of power, as the twinship may alleviate the loss of a sense of individual power. It is common to read about twins who are twice as strong, and get up to all sorts of antics to confuse others and gain advantages over them, particularly in children's books. Books tend to emphasise twins taking refuge in the twinship and twin identity rather than their individual identities.

The twin bond is not only a source of strength and comfort. Many of the themes in twin literature cover the oppressive nature of the twin bond alongside the terror of separation for one or both twins. One of the twins feels suffocated by the enmeshed twin relationship and feels a desperate need to escape, while the other suffers unbearable anxiety at this event. The anxiety generated when twins are separated may be so great that it is often expressed as if the individual self has been rendered apart—an experience also described by some actual twins.

As another common theme, where issues of sameness are explored and the fictional twins together embody an enclosed twin system, the authors describe the life of the twin pair as stagnant, sterile, lacking in development or direction of one or both twins. Sometimes the attempt by one of the twin pair to be free from the twinship will even lead to the death of the other twin, to enable the separating twin to be free and thrive. But sometimes the fictional separated twins wither and die, as if they are unable to live individually.

Twins are felt to embody a sense of eternal duality in all of us. This may be linked with ideas of heaven and earth, as in the myth of Castor and Pollux, where Castor was human and mortal, and Pollux immortal. When Castor was killed in battle, Pollux begged his father Zeus, not to separate them, and eventually Zeus relented and allowed them to remain together, one year in heaven, the other in the netherworld. Lash (1993) suggests, "At the deepest level, Twins exemplify the theological proposition of our hybrid nature: half human, half divine ... the myth indicates … mortal ensoulment of an immortal essence. Body and soul must trade spirit back and forth to ensure their ongoing bond." (p. 60) This pairing of heaven and the netherworld, or life and death, embraces the idea that life is not opposed to death, but that death is part of life. Furthermore, "This implies that death is not merely the absence of life but a counterforce that life needs in order to become what it is." (p. 63)

The theme of sexual rivalry in twins in literature is often posed as a threat to the twinship and therefore to the identity of the twins. Typically, one twin falls in love or marries and the other twin feels deeply abandoned and threatened. In some stories, the twin left out takes the place of the "sexual" twin, impersonates them, either by agreement or by deceit, as if the two are simply interchangeable and the third person would not know the difference. The thorny matter of paternity arises when the woman becomes pregnant after such a swap, an issue that may play a part in certain cultural situations as regards how the twin offspring are viewed as described in Chapter Five.

Twins and doubles

There are links between twins and doubles as they are used in literature. Although I will not go into a detailed exploration of doubles and their significance, I will briefly write about them, because the processes involved in the creation of doubles have some bearing on the way twins are used in literature. Doubles have been used in both fine literature that explores the nature of our duality, and the more popular end of the market where their value depends on horror.

Doubles or doppelgängers have been used in a different way from twins in literature, and are often felt to have a more threatening and enigmatic quality. Doubles tend to personify the unconscious parts of the mind being enacted, often in dark ways. Doubles may represent instinctual aspects of the self that are usually mediated in the social world by the ego, but in literature they are able to function freely, unfettered by social convention and niceties. In some stories the double steals the identity of the protagonist in ways that are disorientating and disconcerting, and that might become deadly.

In the late eighteenth century, doubles were used in literature more frequently than they are now, to express the destructive split-off aspects of the character. Doubles are felt to be duplicitous and unsettling, possible harbingers of death. They rely on the psychological device of splitting of the self, and the disowning and lack of recognition of the other unwanted aspect of the self. This split usually results in the ultimate downfall or death of the character, especially if the double is killed by a vengeful protagonist.

In more current writing, doubles are more frequently used in a search for identity, or as a benign projected aspect of the self as in Philip Pullman's trilogy, *His Dark Materials* (1995). Both the old and the new uses of the double, or other self, echo the structuring of the mind—the unconscious, more turbulent and ruthless parts, with some elements that are very close to the heart of our identity projected into the double; and the more conscious aspects of the self that attempt to regulate our inner selves while at the same time dealing with outside reality. This is reflected in the tensions and battles between the double and the self in literature.

Sigmund Freud (1919h) described the double as a creation meant to insure us against the destruction of the ego by an energetic denial of the fact and power of death. He suggested that the first double is the immortal soul, which is a split-off aspect of the person separated from the mortal body. With this split, the actuality of death is denied because it is believed that the soul will be preserved in heaven (as with Castor and Pollux). This is a narcissistic solution to the fear of death, as is the creation of a phantasy twin, of which I have already written. The phantasy twin preserves, in the imagination, the longed-for unity with the mother's breast in the moments of pleasure, and denial of the inevitable separation of baby from breast, and the deferment, perhaps, of the fear of annihilation in this separation.

The first double is the phantasy twin. The double as a threatening character is a later development of the split-off aspects of self, and it is a reversal of the idea of an immortal soul held in the loving embrace of God. The threatening double is the result of the projection of violent and unpleasant aspects of oneself or one's experience, and can never be truly vanquished as it is still part of us and the only true resolution would be the reintegration of the split-off parts of the self. The threatening double comes to be felt as threatening as it clamours to be recognised and owned, as the split is undone. As much of the literature on doubles makes clear, the defensive ego projects aspects of the self as if they were foreign to itself, unrecognised and disowned, but enacting something of ourselves. The double then becomes an object of terror. Freud also added that the capacity for self-observation and self-criticism is a manifestation of doubling of the self in a more benign and potentially helpful way.

The longing for perfect understanding and containment, based on very early experiences with mother, as I have described in Chapter One, leads to splitting and projection with the creation of the phantasy twin. Where that early experience is blissful and robust, and gradually leads to the development of a secure sense of identity, the split-off projections will be benign, loving, an ideal twin. At other times, and when circumstances are poor, the infant will cope by projecting the unsatisfied miserable, maybe murderous, feelings she has, creating a threatening double. The identity membrane of infancy is so much less developed and more porous than in most adults, that it is not surprising that the experiences of babies and young children are sometimes so frightening.

It is interesting therefore that while the twins in children's literature are usually portrayed as bound together and adding to the repertoire of strategies of the children to manage their lives, the monsters in books and films represent the split-off destructive doubles. The enmeshed twins represent the idealised aspects of a narcissistic twinship, while the destructive doubles represent the denigrated, unwanted aspects of the self in a narcissistic solution that defies integration of the different parts of the self. These splits may happen because the unconscious wishes are so powerful that it is difficult to contain them, and as they are projected into a double, they will colour the experience of the double or the other as destructive. So on the one hand we have the unconscious idealised twin, and later the more conscious helpful imaginary friends; and on the other are the frightening unconscious aspects of the self as reflected in a double.

In the nineteenth century, the period of Romanticism, a number of books were written about just such a damaging double—Edgar Allen Poe's *William Wilson* (1839b), Fyodor Dostoevsky's *The Double* (1846), Robert Louis Stevenson's *The Strange Case of Dr Jekyll and Mr Hyde* (1886), James Hogg's *The Private Memoirs and Confessions of a Justified Sinner* (1824), to name a few. Nicolas Royle (2014) suggests that in the late eighteenth and early nineteenth century, an accentuated experience of self-consciousness led to a new concept of the self. This was evident in the work of the poets Wordsworth and Coleridge, and also in Rousseau and Goethe. In these works, the double was a projected demonic, disturbed conception of the dark side of the self, mixing ideas of hallucination and reality.

We see this too in Oscar Wilde's *The Picture of Dorian Gray* (1890). Dorian Gray, drawn into a hedonistic lifestyle of pleasure and excess, decides to sell his soul in order to live a pleasure-laden, guilt-free life. He manages to do so by projecting his evil self onto a full-length portrait of himself so that the picture, rather than he, will age and show the ravages of his dissolution, while he remains physically beautiful and unscathed. Dorian pursues a libertine life of depraved, callous, and amoral experiences, causing pain and devastation without care or remorse, and all the while his portrait ages and records all his shocking soul-corrupting sins. Ultimately he has to face and own his alter ego, his portrait, and his sins. He crumbles as he does so.

The creation of twins and doubles in literature as a form of splitting or fragmentation of the mind is not necessarily destructive, as in the horrifying doubles described above. Modern writing has focused ideas of such splitting more on the personality and on the nature of identity, as explored through doubles and multiple identities. They may be unnerving but are not necessarily so. Paul Auster's *New York Trilogy* (1987), particularly the middle novel, *Ghosts*, uses the idea of doubles to express just such shifting and enigmatic identities that merge and fade.

An alter ego may also be regarded as a close and supportive companion, such as the "daemons" in Philip Pullman's trilogy (*His Dark Materials*, 1995), or as imaginary companions that are so frequently used in childhood to provide support at times of developmental stress. Philip Pullman uses daemons in the form of animals to express an aspect of the essential self of his characters. A daemon may be defined as a spirit, or immaterial being, that holds a middle place between people and deities in pagan mythology (echoing the myth of the divine twins). But it has also been defined as one's personal genius, a tutelary spirit, or internal voice.

In these stories, daemons are an expression of the soul, an inner self. Daemons represent the unconscious or preconscious part of the self that emerges to become known at times. The daemons of the children change form frequently, reflecting the unsettled sense of identity of the child and the gradual development of the sense of self. They express the volatility of childhood emotions and understanding. The settling of daemon into its permanent form with maturity represents a firming up of identity. Pullman described the daemon as "that part of you that helps you grow towards wisdom" (2009, p. 5). This device depicts an inner dialogue, a dialogue with the self, based on the development of a sense of otherness. It involves the ability to observe others and oneself while still being oneself, as we develop.

When thinking about the terror of separateness that twins experience, what came to my mind was Philip Pullman's description of the horrors that occur in the evil laboratories in Bolvanger. Pullman described how captured children are taken to a special laboratory where they are separated from their daemons using a unique silver guillotine. The process is called "intercision", and what remained was a "severed child". We encounter one severed child clutching a piece of dried fish. Without his daemon he is unable to live. He is like a ghost child hanging onto the dried fish as a last crumb of comfort before he dies. As the chief character Lyra describes it, "A human being with no daemon was like someone without a face, or with their ribs laid open and their heart torn out: something unnatural and uncanny that belonged to the world of night-ghasts, not the waking world of sense." (p. 215) Or as Thomas Ogden (2005) might describe it, a child in the grip of a night terror, an experience that can't be dreamt, from which they can neither wake nor sleep, but remain evermore in the world of the unborn.

I think we might see "intercision" as a metaphor for the experience in enmeshed twins of the shocking sense of intrusion by the outside world into the twin relationship, and for all twins by the severing of the narcissistic aspects of their relationship as they move to become individuals who are also twins. This development creates terror at the loss of a narcissistic twin haven by separation of the twins, and their fear about their ability to survive alone. This is a theme we encounter frequently in the literature on twins, as I will explore below. The loss of the twin or double threatens the individual with the annihilation of the self.

One aspect, then, of why doubles are unnerving, is what they stand for, what aspects of the personality they represent. Where they represent a destructive or manipulative aspect of the personality, they can be horrifying and are seen as evil. They are at the other end of the spectrum from the supposed at-oneness of twins. The idealisation of the twin or double and the demonisation of it are two opposing aspects of the narcissistic twin relationship that are reflected in the literature and, as we saw in Chapter Five, in cultural practices. They thus represent two sides of the coin based on splitting of the self. What is frequently emphasised in literature is the idea that for each twin, the other twin is perceived as the other self, the alter ego, despite being a separate person—a stereotype based on a narcissistic version of the twin relationship.

In literature as in life, our fascination with twins represents the longed-for haven of a perfect soulmate, based on an idealisation of the early bond with mother and projection of this into the twin relationship. The sense of uncanniness of the double and the premonition of ill to come, of the horror and violence of the discovery of a double of oneself who has stolen our identity, represents the extreme splitting of the self. This experience seems to presage emotional breakdown, as does the separation of the idealised enmeshed twins. Both these states of mind have a deep foundation in the relationship with the mother, and this too is represented in the literature.

Splitting of the self is a profound experience because it occurs unconsciously at times of great vulnerability, and when experiences cannot be understood in verbal or logical terms, but are experienced and continue to exist at sensate levels. This very deep sense of attachment, and terror at the loss of it, has been well expressed in some of the literature and makes a gripping read because it echoes for all of us.

I will look at some of the literature that illuminates various themes by using doubles or twins.

The Prince and the Pauper (1881) by Mark Twain, is a story about two different boys who are identical doubles rather actual twins. I have included it here because in this story, these two boys appear as twins, and represent two aspects of the self that has become divided. It is unlike other stories where a double takes another's place and where no one else but the protagonist sees the double.

The story tells of two boys who look so alike that no one can tell them apart, but who represent two sides of one principle—extreme poverty and brutality, versus extreme wealth of a prince or king and obsequious civility and concern. "Same hair, eyes, voice and manner, form and stature, face and countenance ... Will any of the land maintain that there can be two, not of one blood and birth, so marvellously twinned?" (p. 29) One is a Prince of Poverty, the other a Prince of Limitless Plenty. In the accidental exchange of roles, they learn to adopt each other's personas. In the end they return to their old selves, and essential goodness prevails as each participant takes the lessons he has learned back to his own life.

The story dwells on the inter-changeability and sameness of the two boys despite differences in class and lifestyle, and the fact that they are two very separate individuals. They know of their separateness and difference, but all around them see them as identical.

Mark Twain wrote another book about doubles at two ends of the spectrum in *Pudd'nhead Wilson* (1894). In this story the two boys change places and look so alike that no one notices. One is the son of a slave and therefore at least partly black, the other of a wealthy man. The slave mother of one baby exchanges him for the landowner's white baby when the slaves are sold down the river as punishment for stealing. She does this to protect her own son and give him a life of privilege. Unlike the good that prevails in a similar exchange in *The Prince and the Pauper*, the replacement child (the slave child) brought up by the land-owner turns bad and murders someone. Eventually the rightful heir is restored his place, but he has a miserable life because he feels out of place amongst white people, having been raised as a black person.

Mark Twain uses twins or doubles to highlight the extremes in soci-ety and the difficulty in integrating both aspects of the self or society into a harmonious unit. The stories also represent the difficulty accom-modating the split-off aspects of the self.

Twins in literature are most often used to express a stereotyped view of twins, emphasising their apparent sameness and inter-changeability, creating confusion and mistaken identities. Overall most books support the view that twins have separate and different identities but are still crucially bound to varying degrees by the deep unconscious twin relationship.

Despite some very fine writing about twins, literature often depicts the least interesting, least subtle aspect of twins and dualities. While some novels about twins are written by authors who are twins, many are not, and this raises a question about the extent to which authors who are singletons can really understand the intricacies and nuances of twin relationships. There are many books that are really rather crude stories about twin capers, which use the device of twins for dramatic effect rather than depth of character. However, there are some that delve much deeper into twin relationships and matters of identity.

Issues of identity and individuality in separated twins

I will look in some detail at a few of the books I have read that exem-plify how we view twin relationships and the nature of identity. Some of the books have expressed something of the deeper nature of the twin relationship and have used the twin relationships to promote a deeper understanding.

George Sand first described twins in the nineteenth century, in *La Petite Fadette*, translated as *Fanchon the Cricket* (2012). But earlier still, Shakespeare wrote two plays about twins that tapped into both the common ideas about twins—their looking so alike as to be indistinguishable and usually mistaken for each other, as in *A Comedy of Errors* and *Twelfth Night*; and also the deeper more subtle aspects of their relationship with each other, such as the deep bond between twins and their profound longing for each other when separated.

Shakespeare's twins

Shakespearian twins have an intense bond, one that exceeds that of other siblings. Judging by his works and their connection with his own life, Shakespeare was fascinated by twins and doubling, and he used his insights and extraordinary literary ability to express his ideas, and to build and create works of deep psychological and emotional experiences.

Both Shakespeare himself and the many works he created have stirred an incredible industry of descriptive, critical, and analytical work—about his existence and the relevance of his writing, both in the context of his time and the current day—treatises and papers of variable quality and veracity. Although personal details about him were not on record, the main events in his life and the contours of it are well documented in parish, municipal, and commercial archives. He used his life experiences to dramatic effect in his plays, though we cannot claim to know the man through his works. But artists reveal themselves and leave residues in their work that can help us know more about their unconscious processes.

Shakespeare was the father of twins, Hamnet and Judith, named after close friends, Hamnet and Judith Sadler. Hamnet, Shakespeare's only son, died when he was eleven years old, probably of the plague. His elder daughter Susanna, and the surviving twin, Judith, both lived to marry and bear children, though the only grandchild to survive into adulthood was Elizabeth, the daughter of Susanna.

Shakespeare used his own life experiences to deepen his characterisation. Although nothing is known about Shakespeare's experience of grief over Hamnet's death, it may be that he was expressing something of his own feelings when he wrote in *King John* (1596):

Constance cries:

Grief fills the room up of my absent child,
Lies in his bed, walks up and down with me,

> Puts on his pretty looks, repeats his words,
> Remembers me of all his gracious parts,
> Stuffs out his vacant garments with his form;
> Then, have I reason to be fond of grief?
> Fare you well: had you such a loss as I,
> I could give better comfort than you do.
> I will not keep this form upon my head,
> When there is such disorder in my wit.
> O Lord! my boy, my Arthur, my fair son!
> My life, my joy, my food, my all the world!
> My widow-comfort, and my sorrows' cure!
>
> (*King John* 3, 4, 1479–1491)

There has been debate about whether the death of Hamnet prompted Shakespeare to write *Hamlet*. Perhaps Shakespeare's grief over the death of his son lies at the heart of the tragedy of *Hamlet*, a play in which doubles and doubling play a significant part. However, the majority of scholars disagree with this idea. It may be that Hamnet's death prompted the writing of *Twelfth Night*, a play in which a girl twin believes her twin brother has died, drowned at sea in a storm.

Shakespeare used the theme of "twinning" or doubling in many of his plays but only two plays feature twins per se as a central theme, *The Comedy of Errors* (1594) and *Twelfth Night* (1601). They were the first and last plays he wrote.

Shakespeare visited the Inns of Court several times, performing his plays and generally hobnobbing with the members of the Inns and the students. Many of his plays use themes relating to the law. One aspect of this, mistaken identity, is a recurring theme in his plays, and probably had significance in the courts of the day. He used twins for both comic effect and apparently as a teaching guide for the audiences of members of the Inns of Court. Both *The Comedy of Errors* and later *Twelfth Night* were performed at, and received with particular interest and excitement, in the Inns of Court.

In English law, the concept of "reasonable doubt" is of significance in proving a defendant guilty or innocent. Where there might be doubt about the identity of the defendant, as with "identical" twins, mistaken identity could lead to errors of judgment and punishment of the innocent. It is thought that *The Comedy of Errors* was used as teaching material for the law students, to alert them to this issue, and perhaps also to emphasise the differences between even so-called "identical" twins. Current research on

DNA testing may now offer a solution to this problem. Important findings in the detailed identification of DNA have enabled the police to identify suspects, distinguishing them from their MZ twins using their genetic profile and the fact that even MZ twins do not have identical genetic profiles.

In both of these plays, the twins are separated by a storm at sea and later reunited. The loss of the other twin creates unbearable longing and the consequent search for the lost twin. In both plays mistaken identity and the consequences of this confusion is a central feature.

The Comedy of Errors was written two years before Hamnet died in 1596. It features twin brothers, both named Antipholus—one of Ephesus, the other of Syracuse. They have twin servants, both named Dromio, bought by their father, Aegeon, when his twin boys were born. When the father and his wife were sailing back to Syracuse with their twin sons and their twin servants, a storm wrecked their ship. They were rescued by two separate ships, and the twin sons were split up, each with their twin servant, eventually arriving in a different city—one pair in Ephesus, the other in Syracuse.

Antipholus of Syracuse longs for his lost twin brother and after eighteen years he set out to look for him, visiting many countries in his search. He is a romantic wanderer, sensitive and introspective. In contrast Antipholus of Ephesus is smug and self-satisfied, and a hotheaded businessman, whose impetuous behaviour creates conflict around him. It is in part his difficulty in resolving issues that later results in Antipholus of Ephesus being perceived as insane, when the twins are eventually reunited and the confusion around them multiplies.

The characters of other twins in the play are also very different. Dromio of Ephesus is clownish and reserved, while Dromio of Syracuse is a clever talkative joker. As twins often do, they argue about which twin is older and who should exit first, but finally, in a compromise that does not resolve the conflict, they decide to leave together.

Antipholus of Syracuse clearly expresses the depth of the bond between the twins and the feeling of being utterly bereft at their separation, when he says:

> I am to the world like a drop of water
> That in the ocean seeks another drop
>
> (*The Comedy of Errors* 1, 2, 35–36)

He experiences the prolonged separation as a psychical rupture, one in which he feels he has lost part of his self. However, Antipholus of

Ephesus does not seem to experience his separation from his twin brother nearly as intensely. He hardly seems aware of his loss, having established a full and busy life for himself. This theme of one twin with an intense longing while the other does not feel bothered by the separation is common in the literature.

No one in Ephesus was aware that there were two identical-looking men called Antipholus, and two identical servants called Dromio. Consequently when Antipholus of Syracuse arrives in Ephesus, confusion reigns, identities are mistaken, and here the comedy of errors begins as the two sets of twins are repeatedly mistaken for each other. The comic absurdities expose the different values and concerns of each individual twin, and the nature of individual identity is explored as a central theme in this play. The dramatic tension is created around the two sets of twins, as the author plays with illusion and reality, and creates conflict and disorder in their lives.

Order can only be restored when the truth about their identities has been established and the individual realities are faced. The integrity of the individual identities of each twin is of central importance. The clear differences between the twins, despite their similar appearances, highlights their unique individuality, and unlocks the stereotype of twins as indistinguishable from each other. Shakespeare introduces differences alongside the similarities between the twin brothers, and the repeated mixing up of the twins by others highlights these differences as they all eventually emerge from the confusion.

A more complex dramatic structure is created in *Twelfth Night*. Sebastian and Viola are opposite-sex twins who look so alike they are able to pass for each other.

A bewildered Count Orsino says:

> One face, one voice, one habit and two persons,
> A natural perspective that is and is not.
>
> (*Twelfth Night* 5, 1, 216–217)

And Antonio, equally puzzled, when he encounters Viola (who has disguised herself as Cesario) and Sebastian, says:

> How have you made division of yourself?
> An apple, cleft in two is not more twin
> Than these two creatures. Which is Sebastian?
>
> (*Twelfth Night* 5, 1, 233–234)

Separated at sea in a shipwreck, Viola and Sebastian get caught up in a tangled web of love and disguise. Viola is rescued from the shipwreck and lands on Illyria, having been separated from Sebastian. She disguises herself as a boy to fend for herself, and she calls herself Cesario. She works as a page for Count Orsino, with whom she falls in love. However, Count Orsino is in love with Olivia, and Viola/Cesario is dispatched to woo Olivia for the Count. Olivia falls in love with Cesario/Viola, believing her to be a man. A complicated love triangle ensues.

Viola's twin brother Sebastian is also rescued from the shipwreck. He too lands on Illyria and is befriended by Antonio, who is a man wanted for former acts of piracy against Count Orsino. Antonio remains a staunch companion and protector of Sebastian. Both twins thus get involved with Count Orsino's court. There is much confusion of identities as Viola/Cesario and Sebastian interact with the other characters at the court, and, as in *The Comedy of Errors*, this causes mayhem and conflict. Finally, Viola and Sebastian meet up again in a joyful reunion, and everything is resolved. Allegiances change, reparations are made, and in the end, Viola marries Count Orsino, and Sebastian marries Olivia.

Twelfth Night explores not only the consequences of mistaken identity, but also the themes of split-off aspects of the self, especially those of masculinity and femininity. Rustin and Rustin (2004) suggest that Shakespeare expresses the bisexual aspects of identity through the twins Viola and Sebastian, as they explore the differences between men and women. Although they look so alike, they are very different characters. Whereas Viola is passionate, caring, and reflective, Sebastian is shallower. They also suggest that the fact that Viola has a twin brother with whom she has shared years of intimacy has enabled her to impersonate a male figure more easily than would a young woman who is a singleton. "In a male disguise, she can explore the split off male aspects of herself previously contained in her twin brother." (pp. 118–119)

In both *Twelfth Night* and *The Comedy of Errors*, the differences between the twins can be seen as split-off and disowned aspects of each other. As already discussed, this process is an internal individual mechanism that is used to manage unwanted or uncomfortable aspects of the self. For twins it is more complex because of the presence of another actual twin, and they may reach a compromise by dividing up attributes between them, accepting the other twin's projections, in their struggle for individuality and difference.

Like Antipholus of Syracuse, when Sebastian and Viola are separated in the storm and shipwreck, they express their intense longing and pain, feeling as if they are inseparable to the depths of their souls. The clarity and depth of the writing about this indicates Shakespeare's understanding of the deep, sensate, unconscious twin bond that exists in all twin pairs. Sebastian and Viola are bound in a loving twinship, and since their parents have died, they would have relied on each other even more as they mourn them. Unsurprisingly their reunion at the end of the play has a profound emotional impact.

Sebastian and Viola are one of the few examples of opposite-sex twins in literature, and they are so closely bound to each other and so alike in appearance, it seems that Shakespeare wrote about them as if they were "identical" twins. Perhaps they reflected his perceptions of his own twin children, Judith and Hamnet, based on his personal longings for a twin. It is thought that Shakespeare did not have a great deal of contact with his children, as he was so often away, acting and earning money in London. So he would not have spent much time with them, and would have understood their relationship from his own internal longings. Perhaps his ideas about twinship, especially in *Twelfth Night*, reflect his own phantasies about the nature and closeness of the twin bond and the sense of longing for a twin.

Identity and individuality in enmeshed twin brothers

Le Petite Fadette (1849) by George Sand, later translated into English as *Fanchon the Cricket*, is a charming story about male twins, Landry and Sylvinet, living in rural France in the nineteenth century. It captures the essence of the twin relationship and the difficulties for twins in achieving an optimum degree of separation from each other. It examines superstition in relation to twins, as well as real issues in raising them.

The twins, Landry and Sylvinet, appear so similar that the midwife makes a mark on the wrist of one to distinguish them, though the mother never has difficulty in recognising which twin she is dealing with. The father fears that they will become so close that they will be inseparable, so that if they part, one or both may die; or that one may be so consumed with grief at the death of the other, that he too would die. The parents are advised to separate and distinguish the twins from each other while they are still young. They are told to treat twins as individuals and not dress them alike. But they ignore this advice, as the twins want to dress alike.

The twin boys are very close, always play together, and imitate each other. They cannot be divided and always share and support each other. But it emerges that they are two distinct individuals and they express their individuality within the twin bond. Landry is robust physically and mentally, able to relate to others, and goes out to work, taking pleasure in what he does well. Sylvinet, on the other hand, is more delicate than Landry, and he languishes in Landry's shadow. He finds the separateness between them unmanageable and lies around at home pining away, drawing the whole family into his suffering. Everyone has to tend to and accommodate him.

When Landry goes away to work, Sylvinet's deep longing for Landry grows, and as Landry flourishes, Sylvinet comes to feel his love is unrequited. Sylvinet's despairing feelings about Landry turn into dislike, then into hate and spite, as Landry does not return to the enmeshed twinship that Sylvinet craves. Sylvinet is not able to acknowledge Landry's deep love and concern for him, as he is too narcissistically engrossed with Landry to really love him as a separate person.

Landry meets and falls in love with Fanchon, who lives in the woods with her grandmother and a crippled younger brother, in an impoverished and very harsh home. Initially Landry is afraid of and despises Fanchon, but gradually he comes to see her goodness and beauty, and he falls in love with her. Landry hides this love from Sylvinet for fear of hurting him, and also from the family because they would not consider Fanchon good enough for them.

Inevitably the affair becomes known. Sylvinet is deeply wounded by Landry's attachment to Fanchon, and seems at times to be on the verge of death in his jealousy and despair at losing Landry to Fanchon. He plays on this to keep his brother captive and his family in thrall to him. The family is desperate and asks Fanchon, who is a natural herbalist, to help Sylvinet. She cures him using her psychological understanding of the situation and bolsters his sense of himself, while warning him to stop manipulating the family with his supposed weakness.

Fanchon has emerged as a clever, beautiful, and wealthy young woman, a suitable match for Landry, and he marries her. After his initial intense hostility towards her, Sylvinet also falls in love with Fanchon, and he deals with this impasse by absenting himself completely. He enlists as a soldier to serve in the Napoleonic wars, an occupation in which he shows himself to be a strong man and in which he achieves distinction.

While the mysterious nature of twin love in this story excites all the characters, people identify the twins without difficulty and treat them as individuals. There is little play on inter-changeability of the characters as they are too different in personality, and they come to look different as their lives diverge. The superstition that if one twin leaves the other will die is refuted. The complexity of twin relationship is recognised, as is the lasting deep narcissistic bond between the twins.

Some authors use the device of the twin relationship to express dual aspects of themselves. Patrick White states in his autobiography (1981) that the twin brothers, Waldo and Arthur Brown, in *The Solid Mandala* (1966) represent two halves of himself. "Waldo is myself at my coldest and worst." (White, 1982, pp. 146–147, quoted by Juliana de Nooy, 2005, p. 28)

Juliana de Nooy, in her comprehensive study of twins in literature and the arts, states that this is the first novel written about twins who live out their lives together, and that it was followed by Tournier and Chatwin (see below). This book describes a lethal, sterile bond between two male twins, a relationship that allows no other relationships to exist without damage to one twin. They can't survive alone but suffocate in their relationship.

The twin brothers, though very different in character, live out their lives together as a couple. Waldo is supposedly the clever, educated twin, while Arthur presents himself as a bumbling fool, but in fact appears to be an idiot savant, secretly reading Dostoyevsky and other illuminating texts, much to Waldo's disapproval. While Waldo longs for contact with others, particularly his neighbour Dulcie, he is unable to relate to anyone other than Arthur. Arthur, on the other hand, manages to make loving relationships with various women in their lives.

Waldo and Arthur remain tied to each other in a life that has no future or context other than the relationship they have within the twin-ship. It was "more than habit, Waldo considered bitterly, which made them one." (p. 24) There is a suggestion that they also have a sexual relationship: "they shared secrets warmer than appeared" (p. 28). They were deeply bound together: "in some ways you were so close you did not notice" (p. 31). The twinship is the central core of their existence. They live into old age in a state of mutual stagnation, bound together in a narcissistic twin relationship. Waldo feels persecuted by Arthur but is unable to separate from him. He feels Arthur's existence as a wound. And they are "fused by consent at some points. Waldo is the one who takes the lead. Joining them together at the hand. And because Waldo needed it that way, only the knife could sever it." (p. 256)

Arthur's hatred of Waldo is stifled by his need for his twin, and he is a more loving personality. Arthur is more able to negotiate a balance between the twinship and relationships with others. He uses symbols to represent the various relationships in his life—symbols that he finds in glass marbles and which he sees as solid mandalas. (A mandala is a circular figure representing the universe.) To Arthur, "The mandala is a symbol of totality ... Its protective circle is a pattern of order superimposed on psychic chaos." (p. 238)

Arthur keeps several of these marbles that represent different people important to him, relating to different relationships in his life. The one he keeps for himself as representing his inner world has a double spiral that can "knit and unknit reasonably" (p. 280), "a coil of green and crimson circlets" (p. 228). This pattern represents his ability to enter and leave relationships, including that with Waldo, without a sense of utter devastation. Waldo's mandala, in contrast, has a knot at its centre, which Arthur realised was the whole point as it represented Waldo "born with his innards twisted" (p. 32). Arthur sensed that Waldo would never untie the knot, even though in certain lights, the tortuously interwoven knot at the centre of the marble would dissolve for a moment. Waldo was bound in the hated twin relationship, unable to find a separate space for himself, only able to separate from his twin by death or murder.

Waldo becomes very ill. As his end approaches, Waldo destroys his life's work in hatred for his twin brother and himself. Arthur sees Waldo on his deathbed, and recognises the hatred Waldo has always directed at all living things, especially him, and particularly at a poem Arthur had written that celebrated their common pain. Arthur recognises that Waldo is trying to kill him by burning his poem and all their papers, and he feels that he is responsible for Waldo's hatred of him. Arthur believes he had bred in Waldo the hatred Waldo was preparing to die of. He feels that he, not Waldo, is to blame for their miserable entrapment and life. He was the getter of pain. "Then Waldo, in the agony of their joint discovery, reached out and grabbed him by the wrist, to imprint him forever with the last moment." (p. 294)

So even in the death of one of them, the twin brothers remain narcissistically attached, both physically and emotionally. Arthur runs away in fear after Waldo's death. He does not believe he could live without his twin brother, as Waldo was more than half of him. He believes that he, Arthur, should have died at birth. He feels Waldo had known this, when it was too late, when he was dying.

These twins represent the deathliness of an enmeshed twin relationship that allows no individuality, where there is such murderous hatred by one twin that it poisons them both. Even after death the surviving twin cannot free himself of the strangling twinship.

There are several parallels between *The Secret Mandala* and Michel Tournier's *Gemini* (1975). In both, the twin relationship is seen as stifling and sterile, but also as the source of stability and identity for the twin pair. There is also a link in the symbolism used: for Patrick White it is the round marble with its whirling internal coils that represents the mandala, the soul of each twin; for Michel Tournier it is the ovoid geminate cell of the twins entwined inextricably with each other. But whereas each mandala represents individuality for each twin within the twin relationship, the ovoid geminate cell represents the twin pair bound together as two halves of one. In *Gemini*, the twin pearls that are acquired by their uncle, Alexandre, are symbolic of this twin relationship—individually they are worthless, but together are extremely valuable.

Michel Tournier's *Gemini* (1975) is an intriguing book that gets to the heart of a narcissistic twinship. I have used a number of quotes from the book as Tournier clearly describes his idealised view of the twinship and also its dangers and restrictions.

Jean and Paul are twins born into a large loving family. The twins are the last children to be born. Their mother, Marie-Barbara, is aware that asleep, they revert

> to their most private selves, reduced to what is their *common denominator*—they are indistinguishable. It is the same body entwined with its double, the same visage with the same lowered eyelids presenting at once its full face and its right profile, the one chubby and tranquil, the other pure and clear-cut, and both entrenched in a mutual rejection of everything outside the other. (ibid., p. 11)

In the sterile, stultifying, stifling bond of twin relationship, all life and love external to it is killed.

Tournier defines the parameters of the twin relationship as he sees it and as it unfolds in this book. For "identical" twins, writes Tournier, the usual determinants of heredity and environment are combined with something else—a bit of the environment is embedded in a homogeneous heredity. This is both a mutilation and it also allows "air and light and noise into the inmost privacy of being. Real twins are a single entity with the monstrous faculty of occupying two different positions in space. But the space which divides them is of a special kind" (p. 415), a rich and vital intergeminate space, the extended soul, which is infinitely extensible. Twinless people wander in "a barren desert" in comparison.

As they grow up, it is as if Jean and Paul embody the conflict between individual identity and engagement with the world and productivity versus the stagnation and deathliness of undifferentiated twin relationship. Enclosure within the narcissistic bubble of twin relationship is glorified, and the ordinary productive relationships of individuals are denigrated as inferior to the richness of the twinship. In their childhood, the twin boys are both called Jean-Paul and they act as one.

At night they performed rituals to strip away the residues of their separate days, glorified as an act of purification or exorcism, stripping away "all external influences, every alien accretion, in order that each might return to the sheet anchor that his twin brother was to him, and this effort, if we performed it together at one and the same time was directed chiefly toward the other, each one purifying and cleansing his twin, to make him identical to himself" (p. 195). Through this ritual, each twin "has dropped back into his mold—which is his twin" (p. 130). "Geminate communion has us head to tail in the same ovoid position as the double foetus. This position expresses our determination not to become involved in the dialectic of life and time." (p. 278)

This purification ritual was called the game of Bep and consisted of "cryptophasia, Aeolian, stereophony, stereoscope, geminate intuition, ovoid loving and its preliminary exorcism, praying head to tail, seminal communion" (p. 196). This process, like their twinship, was idealised and reinforced the idea that as twins they were superior to singletons who could never approach this level of intimacy. "The massive pleasures of the geminate embrace are to the acidulated joys of twinless coupling like those fat sweet juicy greenhouse fruits compared to the little sharp wild berries whose tartness contains all the Mountain and forest." (p. 199)

They call their twin communication "Aeolian" which "starts from the silence of visceral communion and rises to the verge of speech used by society, but without ever reaching it" (p. 133). It is an absolute dialogue addressed only to an identical twin, "a language without diffuseness, radiating nothing, the concentration of everything that was most private and secret in us—rooted in the common visceral mass to which we both belonged". This preverbal communication would represent the deep sensate bond between the twins.

Paul believed that, as twins, he and Jean were never lonely and that any single child, born without a twin, would always be lonely and could never recover from this. He sees twins as innocents whereas singletons are murderers who have killed and eaten their twin in utero. He never wanted a teddy bear because he believed he already had one, a live one, his twin brother. Thus we can see that for Paul, Jean is the embodiment and concretisation of a phantasy twin. Where a single child projects a phantasy twin onto a teddy or doll, it at the same time creates space for development and individuality. In contrast Paul clings to a concrete version of his phantasy twin.

However, in adolescence their encasement in a twin shell excluding outside life and relationships began to change. Tournier identifies the tensions between the twins that both keep them enslaved in the twinship but also create the desperate wish by one of them to be separate. He identifies each twin's own sphere of individuality within the twin relationship by the different characters with their own particular needs and desires. Paul is confident, wilful, and autocratic. Jean is restless, open, and inquisitive. Jean strives to extricate himself from the twinship at all costs, and Paul seeks to maintain the geminate structure, again at all costs.

Within the rigid geminate world, there is no personal choice, purpose, or free will. Everything that happens is part of the geminate structure, and it is fated to happen. In Jean's desperation to get out of this geminate prison, he uses his girlfriend to break the stifling bond between them. But Paul feels that "when one has experienced the intimacy of twinship, no other intimacy can be felt as anything but a disgusting promiscuity" (p. 190).

To Jean the geminate cell is the opposite of being, the negation of time, history, of everything that happens, the vicissitudes that are the price of living. Between an unchanging stillness and living impurity, Jean chooses life rather than geminate paradise. Jean leaves to travel the world and as the twin brothers become dispaired, Jean gains his freedom but Paul suffers unbearably. Paul sets out to find his brother by retracing every step Jean has taken, as if to live the experiences that Jean has had and to reunite himself with Jean. Paul begins to achieve some degree of engagement with the world as he realises how important it is for him to get everything he can from the journey and not cut any corners. He becomes trapped in East Germany as the wall is built, looking after an elderly woman, and declining the offers of help to escape.

The split Germany is a metaphor for the dispaired twins. Finally Paul makes the perilous journey to escape to the West at the last moment, but the tunnel collapses on his rebirth as a dispaired twin. He is rescued but suffers the amputation of his arm and leg. Jean's freedom and separateness lead to Paul's mutilation. The lost leg and arm become an expression of the sacrifice Paul has made in losing Jean—in allowing Jean to lead his own life. Paul has needed to undergo ritual amputations to reunite him spiritually with Jean. He feels his missing limbs are his missing twin, and that the experience and the pain have created an elastic link to Jean stretching across the world, a link that binds them together again.

Thus, they are cosmically bound together even in their ultimate loss—Jean as a disappeared and dispaired twin, and Paul as the twin who remains bound in his mind to Jean through amputations in his rebirth as a dispaired twin. Paul believes they remain cosmically connected in their intimacy, an extended soul.

Bruce Chatwin, in his novel *On The Black Hill* (1982), explores the changing relationship between twin boys who also share a special intimacy as twins and a very close-knit bond with some of the intensity of Tournier's twins, but with some hope for the future.

Benjamin and Lewis are "identical" twins. As with some of the other books, it is hard to tell the twins apart when they are young. In old age, however, they have become quite different in personality and in appearance. They live together with their mother and father, a harsh life in the farmlands of Black Hill on the Welsh borders. They share a bed and there are intimations of a sexual relationship. Tasks around the farm and home are divided between them—Benjamin was ill as a child and is more delicate. As an adult he is more homely and as his mother's favourite, helps her around the house. Lewis works in the fields and is more robust and outgoing (thus echoing the situation in *La Petite Fadette*).

While their mother is alive, Benjamin and Lewis are portrayed as a sterile pair. Nothing must distinguish or come between them. They swap names for fun. They share everything. They have a secret language "of the angels", and they believe they were born with it. The twin brothers are so close psychically that they know each other's thoughts and there-fore quarrel without speaking. They are in such close communication and so attuned to each other that when Benjamin is injured, Lewis draws the pain from Benjamin and makes it his own. At another time, Lewis starts shivering during a train journey when he senses Benjamin, far away, is lost in the snow and in danger of freezing to death. He races to rescue him, knowing just where to find him. Meanwhile, Benjamin has dragged himself through the snow to the relative safety of a ledge—he imagined he heard his brother shouting in his ear, "I'll die if you go to sleep" (p. 104), and thus pushing him on to safety rather than lying down in the snow to die. And later, when Lewis dies in tractor acci-dent in a distant field, Benjamin is suddenly struck down with a sudden sharp pain in his chest and falls to floor.

It is as if the twins are two parts of one person and they are not able to exist independently. Even the stronger Lewis is always preoccupied with Benjamin. In *The Solid Mandala*, the glass marbles represent the entanglement of the twin relationship, as does the ovoid geminate cell in *Gemini*. In this book eggs are a frequent theme, perhaps representing the closed system of the enmeshed twin relationship, and a return to the idea of an ovum that has split to create two babies, though this link is not as obviously indicated as in the other two books. Eggs are broken when someone is in distress, an indication of the process of pain that must be endured for the twins to establish individuality and separate lives for themselves. There is awareness throughout the book that the twin men need to become separate people for any development to take place in their lives. However, the magnetic pull of the twinship is a constant counterbalance to any move towards individuality. It is only after mother's death that Benjamin and Lewis feel enabled to achieve a degree of psychic separation. It is as if mother kept them in a sterile, bound condition.

Any outsider to the twinship is considered to be a threat. Any move that Lewis makes towards the outside world, and outside the twinship, leads to some sort of collapse in Benjamin. When Lewis leaves to work on another farm, Benjamin believes that Lewis has stolen his soul, and when he looks in the mirror, he sees himself vanishing, as he thinks about killing himself. Benjamin and Lewis hate being mistaken for each other, but they mistake their image in the mirror for other twin. When Lewis becomes involved with a woman, Benjamin is so murderously angry that Lewis has to leave home until the anger subsides. As with the twins in Tournier's *Gemini*, one twin, Lewis, wants to travel, but the other, Benjamin, wants them to stay bound together at home. Separation is unmanageable for Benjamin.

After mother dies they become united by the memory of her, and her death creates changes in their relationship. It allows them to grow and relate to each other in a new and more mature way. They move together into the parental bed, as if they have become a productive, married couple. They do become a new sort of couple, odd though it is, a homosexual couple, one that is idealised in that they see themselves as a pseudo-reproductive pair. Their great-nephew becomes their substitute child and heir, as if they have produced him.

In Tournier's *Gemini*, the twins Jean and Paul have an uncle who is homosexual and who roams the world using encounters with other men to explore and find himself—searching for an ideal soulmate twin and echoing the struggle the twins endure. But in *Gemini*, the sterility of a narcissistic homosexual relationship is exposed. In Chatwin's book, it is as if the twins find a less narcissistic homosexual twinship, one that actually allows for otherness and productivity in relation to it, and a more mature kind of relatedness.

Instead of remaining isolated in the twin relationship, Benjamin and Lewis become involved with others around them, especially their long-exiled sister and her grandson, their great-nephew. They "knew their lives had not been wasted and that time, in its healing circle had wiped away the pain and the anger, the shame and the sterility, and had broken into the future with the promise of new things" (p. 14). Their great-nephew becomes the new hope in their lives, as if he is their child. He becomes a symbol of a new future that emerges from the previously sterile twinship.

Benjamin and Lewis manage their emotions in relation to each other in a more mature and considerate way, and overcome many of the powerful emotions that emerge within over-close relationships. They are not crippled by the murderous hatred we read about in Patrick White's twin brothers. They live together until the grand old age of eighty. Despite Benjamin's refusal of otherness, they manage to live together in relative harmony. After Lewis' death, Benjamin spends an hour each day at his graveside, thus maintaining his psychical communion with his twin brother, while also acknowledging his death. Though they remained enmeshed twins, they could allow a measure of individuality between them.

There is a different feel about twinship in each of these books, though each of them is about enmeshed twin brothers. Some are about MZ twins, others about DZ twins, but all expose the beating heart of the twin relationship and the difficulties twins encounter in finding a degree of separation that can enable each of them to retain a sense of individual identity while still honouring the twin relationship as a primary one. In them we find common themes: identity, soul-sharing, inter-changeability, playing on confusion, and polarities like weak or strong. We also see the common difficulty for one twin in allowing the other to be separate.

Another important example of writing about the twin relationship in a way that explores and deepens our understanding of it and its links with phantasy twins and the eternal search for identity is Agota Kristof's (1997) trilogy, *The Notebook, The Proof, The Third Lie*. The story is never fixed, as it changes with each book in the trilogy, as do the identities and the nature of the relationships of the twin brothers. Like Paul Auster's *New York Trilogy* (1987), there is a sense of shifting and interchangeable identity, leaving us uncertain and searching.

Kristof explores the lethal bond of a twin relationship where there is no loving parental care or intervention. In the first book, *The Notebook*, the life of the twins Lucas and Claus is described in sometimes horrifying detail. After the war breaks out, they are left by their mother with their starkly unloving, punitive grandmother, in a bleak, dirty, and barren house. The only token of ordinary life they have is their father's diction- ary. They are undernourished and have to educate and learn to fend for themselves in order to survive. They keep a daily notebook in which they record their self-corrected examples of absolute objectivity, as they develop their own system of morality. They create themselves through a regimen of mental and physical exercises designed to make them immune to ordinary human emotions and frailties. They toughen their minds and bodies.

The twins Lucas and Claus talk, think, and act as one. They are not normal children and show none of the dependency or relatedness other children engage with. They live in a separate and different twin world of their own. Mother (who visits occasionally) believes they are one and the same person. At father's insistence, they are separated when they first go to school. But this turns out to be a disastrous move—the twins feel: "This distance between us seems monstrous, the pain is unbearable. It is as if they have taken half our bodies away. We can't keep our balance, we feel dizzy, we fall, we lose consciousness." (p. 23) Thereafter they are kept together in the class where they learn reading, writing, and arithmetic.

As a bound twin pair, they live in a totalitarian partnership, based on their own code of ethics and morality—an amoral, duty-bound existence according to their own moral code. They adhere to a rule of "absolute need" which encompasses everything from their need for pencils and paper, and therefore their entitlement to them free from the stationer, to their feeding and caring for their hateful grandmother, for a deserter in the woods, a starving sexually depraved neighbour and her mother, and the priest who molests the girl. With equal duty-bound amorality, they kill without guilt or remorse when asked to do so, such as a woman whose daughter has been raped and murdered, and eventually they kill grandmother at her request after she has suffered a stroke. They claim there is no love and goodness in them, just moral duty.

At the end of *The Notebook*, the twins separate in a deathly manner leaving no hope for aliveness and development. Father has returned, having been tortured, and is asking for help to cross the border into safety. The twins make plans for him to cross the border without any identification, as if to deny their relationship with him. They actually use this plan to enable Claus to cross the border safely to the other country by sending father ahead to take the blast of the mines at the border, and in his death to provide a stepping-stone for Claus to cross unharmed. The sacrifice of father to achieve their separateness is indicative of the mortal blow to development that can take place when such an important move is unmediated by a loving parental figure, internal or external. It is patricide in order to further their own aims, and the consequence is the deathliness of the experience of separation, as the twins do not have a good inner father or mother to help them engage with the outside world.

So in this book, we have deeply enmeshed twins who function as a single unit, and use others and the outside world shamelessly to further their needs, based on their own code of ethics. They are "identical", interchangeable twins who exercise more power as a twin pair than they would as individuals. They use each other to develop a twin system of invulnerability.

In the second book, *The Proof*, we find Lucas searching for his own identity, just existing meaninglessly. Questions begin to emerge about the existence of his missing brother, supposedly a defector to the "other side".

Lucas insists that Claus exists and will come back, and that he won't go to look for him since Claus went away and it is up to him to come back. At the suggestion that he will never come back, Lucas faints.

In this multifaceted complex plot, we find an echo of what is to come regarding the identities of Claus and Lucas when Lucas takes on the responsibility of looking after a crippled child, a relationship in which he deeply identifies with the child. Claus suddenly emerges again, trying to find his twin brother. Peter, an intermediary who knew Lucas when he was fifteen, mistakes Claus for his twin, Lucas. Peter informs Claus that Lucas has left, and he believes Claus is Lucas, that Lucas has returned using a different name. Thus we have the theme of interchangeability and uncertainty about who is who.

When Claus and Lucas separated, they decided it had to be a total separation, not only by a border, but also with no communication between them. After Claus left for the other country, Lucas maintained his entries in the notebooks, and now Peter gives the notebooks, which he has been safeguarding, to Claus. Later, on examination of the notebooks by the authorities, they find that they have been written in the same hand (not two hands as the first book claims), and that the entire text was written in one sequence by one person over a period of not more than six months. They also believe that none of the other characters existed other than the supposed grandmother.

So there is now doubt about whether there were twins at all, a confusion of identities and an enigmatic shifting of identities and facts or non-facts. It is also clear that the notebooks were not written by both twins, but created by one of them, longing for or imagining the lost twin.

In the final book, *The Third Lie*, we have the perspectives of the twins finally coming together, the existence of the twins is confirmed although the relationship is denied by one of them. Claus is again in the old country trying to find his twin. He believes that he (Claus) is seriously ill and dying of a heart complaint. As he waits in his prison cell for his extradition to the new country, he has a dream that awakens memories of his childhood, in a rehabilitation centre, with some mysterious injury. He was a deeply disturbed unpleasant child who caused trouble for all. When the centre was bombed, he was placed with an old woman known as "grandmother".

Is his brother just a dream? Was "father" simply a man wishing to cross the border, who went first so it was safe for Claus to go? Did Claus create a phantasy twin in order to endure the unbearable solitude? It begins to emerge that Claus is not his name, and that the notebooks are all lies, a creation by one person. The new encounter between the twins offers no reconciliation, but a new story is told, linked with his dream, in which Claus is the dispossessed twin. He was accidentally shot by mother, and then left in hospital and disowned. So Claus created a story of his life in the notebooks.

Next we encounter Klaus, a poet in the old country, who writes under a pen name Klaus-Lucas. He remembers the family home in the city with mother and father. There was a row over father's infidelity and mother shot father. The bullet ricocheted and hit his twin, Lucas, in his spine. Lucas was sent to a rehabilitation centre and then abandoned, as mother was in a psychiatric hospital and father was dead. So some of Claus's story is confirmed in Klaus's memory, but it transpires that Claus's real name is Lucas (a transposition of the letters) and that he changed it when he crossed the border. Did Lucas create or live his story?

Klaus rejects Lucas though they both know they are twins. Klaus lives with their now very ill mother. Mother constantly thinks Klaus is Lucas, her abandoned child whom she had injured, her preferred child. Klaus denies that Lucas is his twin though he secretly knows it to be true. He talks to Lucas in his head every night. He tells him that if he is dead, he is lucky—he'd like to be in his place. He got the better deal. His life is so bleak.

Lucas returns to see Klaus again and leaves the notebooks with him. Klaus tries to complete them, again becoming one with Lucas, a coming together of the twins, of diverse aspects of the self, as if they are one. Lucas commits suicide as he is about to be repatriated to other country—although he has been found to be healthy, his twin's denial of his twinship with him and the threat of another total searing separation is unbearable to him. The greater the distance of the separation, the more damaging it is to a resolution of twin relationship.

So we have intertwining characters and stories and truths, and throughout the trilogy there is a theme of shifting identity, essential loneliness, and questions about what twinship might mean; the uncertainty of whether there are twin brothers or whether one is the invention of the other, and which one is the inventor. Were there twins or one lonely child creating a twin to alleviate his loneliness? The twins as a pair are presented as two parts of one whole. Separated, they are bereft and their lives are meaningless, bleak, and hopeless. All other relationships are meaningless to them. The twinship is the great intimacy that binds them: united they function in superior ways; alone they barely exist and always seek intimacy. There can be no reconciliation because the deep wounds, the underlying jealousy and rivalry, are deathly.

The difficulties in developing from deeply narcissistic attachments to individuality are expressed graphically in these books. Both twins remain sterile in their lives: Lucas as a lonely, damaged, desperate, dislocated figure in a foreign world trying to reconnect to his twin for survival; and Klaus umbilically attached to his unloving mother in a bond of devoted hatred and disregard, living a fantasised relationship with the twin he nevertheless refuses to recognise or confirm.

These disturbing books raise questions of identity, self, and other, of the nature of relatedness and love. Belonging, empathy, morality, altruism are all explored. As with the twins in *Gemini*, this story also uses twins to relate the experiences of the brutal division of east and west.

In Thornton Wilder's *The Bridge of St Luis Rey*, written in 1927, we again encounter a lethal bond in a twin relationship in which one twin can't live without the other. Thornton Wilder was himself a twin, whose twin brother died at birth.

> Born prematurely and a twin, he had a precarious start in life. His identical brother [Theophilus], though perfectly formed, was stillborn, too frail to be cried or patted into life, and there was doubt whether Thornton himself would survive. For weeks during that first hot summer he was carried about on a pillow and fed limewater. (Harrison, quoted by Glenn, 1986, p. 627)

Wilder's twinship affected his personality and his writings. Wilder actually connected two of his books with his twinship—*The Bridge of St Luis Rey* (1927) and *Theophilus North* (1973). When he learned about his twin brother's death, he wondered why he had survived, while his brother died. He was not sure whether it was a punishment for something his brother had done, or whether his brother had been allied to God (again a theme of one mortal twin and the other heavenly). He was grateful he had survived, but this led him to feel guilty, as if it was he who had killed his twin brother—a common experience of twins whose other twin dies. He recreated his brother in some of his writings in an attempt to keep him alive. At times he identified with his dead twin brother, so perpetuating his feelings of guilt.

The Bridge of St Luis Rey is a series of short stories that centre around the characters of the people on the bridge when it collapsed. It was a frequently used bridge, and five people died as they were crossing. They plunged into the ravine below, to their deaths. Wilder identified with the people who felt it might have been they who had died on the bridge, and who wondered why it had happened to the five who did die. In the book, Brother Juniper weaves a story about each of the victims of the collapse.

Of the five, one who fell to his death was Esteban, the twin brother of Manuel. Manuel and Esteban are foundling twins, and so alike no one can tell them apart. They speak a secret language that is a symbol of their profound identity with one another. They also use telepathic communication.

Manuel and Esteban work and live together in a closed twinship where they share everything. When Manuel falls in love with an actress, Esteban feels betrayed. Manuel becomes aware of a deep sense of loss as he has an image of Esteban going away, a long way away. This fills him with terror as he realises that all his other attachments in the world are but shadows compared to his twinship with Esteban. Like the twins in *Gemini*, Manuel and Esteban feel that all non-twins are strange and difficult to understand.

Manuel dies of an infection after injuring his leg. Esteban initially assumes Manuel's identity, as if to be united with him again, and he is often assumed by others to be Manuel, as if there was no difference between them. At Manuel's funeral Esteban keeps his distance from the coffin, rather like a magnet in repel mode rather than attract mode, as so often found in the twin bond. He wishes to die to be reunited with Manuel, and in a disguised suicide attempt he runs into a burning building to rescue someone.

Esteban's grief is unmanageable until he meets and shares it with Captain Alvarado who has also suffered a catastrophic loss. Manuel begins to recover and as he starts to make a move to reclaim his life, he falls to his death in the collapse of the ancient bridge. It is as if ultimate success is to be together with his twin in death.

Wilder said a central theme in the book is the fear of catastrophe, and it seems that he believed the birth of himself and his twin was a catastrophe. He linked the date he first gave for the fictional collapse of the bridge with his birthday, but later changed it. Thus, Wilder identified with Esteban, the surviving twin. He used the book to speculate about what it would be like to have a live twin to relate to and do things with, and to recreate the lost twinship that he felt so marked his life. In an idealisation of twinship linked with the loss of his twin, he wrote: "Love is inadequate to describe the tacit, almost ashamed oneness of these brothers." (Wilder, 1927, p. 48)

Glenn (1986) proposes that the experience of Wilder's twinship and the death of his twin at birth have also influenced his other writings, most notably in his book entitled *Theophilus North*. Theophilus was the name of his dead twin, and North is an anagram of the first five letters of Wilder's own first name. It was the last of Wilder's works published during his lifetime. This novel is part autobiography, part the imagined adventure of his twin brother who died at birth. Wilder created an imagined life for his dead twin brother and in a letter to a classmate, wrote: "I was born an identical twin; he lived an hour; if he had survived his name would have been Theophilus … I wrote his memoirs." (Thornton Wilder Society)

Opposite sex twins

The Fall of the House of Usher (1839a) by Edgar Allen Poe is a twin story about opposite sex twins who look very alike. Typically for Poe, it is a dark and mysterious tale.

The narrator is asked to visit an old friend, Roderick Usher, living in a remote and distant place. Usher is ill with a strange disease and needs help. It emerges that his twin sister, Madeline, is also ill and she falls into cataleptic, deathlike trances. Roderick later informs the narrator that his twin sister has died and asks for help placing her in the family tomb. In the coffin, Madeline is noticed as having "the mockery of a faint blush on the bosom and the face and that suspiciously lingering smile upon the lip which is so terrible in death" (ibid., p. 260).

After her "death" Roderick becomes agitated, and without his precious "luminousness of his eye", as if he has lost part of himself. Together they inter Madeline, but Roderick's agitation increases over the next week for no apparent reason. A storm brews and the house begins to glow. The narrator's bedroom is situated directly above the family vault. The narrator attempts to calm Roderick by reading to him aloud, while feeling very edgy himself. As he reads, cracking and ripping sounds are heard somewhere in the house, and then screams, echoing the story he is reading of the screams of a slain dragon.

Roderick becomes increasingly hysterical. He claims that these sounds are being made by his sister, and that they had put her into the tomb alive. The bedroom door is then blown open to reveal the enshrouded, bloodstained figure of Madeline Usher standing there. His twin sister has come back from interment to drag her brother to death with her. They both fall to the floor, dead. The narrator then flees the house and, as he does so, he turns back and sees the House of Usher split in two, as the fragments sink into the lake. The house, identified with the family, collapses as the dynasty ends.

As in *Twelfth Night*, in this story we find the extreme similarity in looks between the twin brother and sister, noticed by the guest after her "death". They also suffer similar mysterious maladies, and are both wasting away. The narrator learns that they "had been twins, and that sympathies of a scarcely intelligible nature had always existed between them" (p. 260).

Poe is thus addressing the intense closeness of the twin bond between these two, and perhaps there is also a suggestion of incest—a theme common in twin literature and beliefs about twins. They live and die together. Perhaps Madeline takes revenge for her twin brother's murderousness in burying her alive. But it is evident in this tale that neither twin can survive alone. It is as if the twins die in the stagnant sterile twin enclosure, twin soulmates who shunned the outside world. They created sameness, suppressed rivalry, and suffocated any sense of individuality. They represent the sterility and deathliness of the enmeshed twin relationship.

In his short story *The Fahrenheit Twins* (2005), Michael Faber investigates the powerful theme of attempts by opposite sex twins to arrest their development in order to preserve the twin relationship as a refuge from a hostile world. The twins are called Marko'cain and Tainto'lilith, creating biblical associations with sinister undertones. Cain killed his brother Abel, and was thus humanity's first murderer. Lilith was Adam's twin or first wife and is associated with evil spirits, God's vengeance in the Book of Isaiah.

The twins live with their scientist parents on a remote Arctic exploration station. They are cast as innocents and spend an apparently idyllic life racing huskies across the frozen tundra, rolling in the snow. The twins collect their mother's sayings and record key events in The Book of Knowledge. They consider this book a sacred object. Their idyllic world is like a paradise and references the Garden of Eden when their mother talks to them about trees that exist beyond "this little paradise". Suddenly, after a research expedition, mother becomes ill and dies.

Father asks the twins how they would like their mother's body to be disposed of. The twins decide to take their mother's body away with them into the wilderness, where they hope to find the right place to bury her. Their father wholeheartedly embraces this plan, and he assists them in preparing for their voyage. The twins set off into the tundra to bury her with meagre rations, on a sled with dogs. In the search to find out what to do with their mother's dead body, the twins discover more about themselves as they travel across the strange land in which they live. They endure life-threatening hazards and a lack of food and water for them and their dogs—clearly a deliberate ploy by their father to get rid of them. On a beach where a helicopter has crashed, the blades wedged in the sand like a cross, they find food to sustain them and the dogs. They believe they have discovered signs to what appears to be a refuge, a tribal tent with a primitive image of their mother on it. They leave her body there on what appears to be a prepared shrine. They believe the universe has directed them there.

In this strange little story, the twins' deeply enmeshed twin bond saves them from a neglectful mother and a father who hates them and finds them an obstacle to the life he wishes to live. The twins endure severe parental neglect and like Agota Kristof's twins, are left to fend for themselves and create a notebook to anchor themselves.

The boy and girl twins are identical in all respects apart from their genitals—identical in their expressions and appearance. In a denial of difference, they claim, "We are the same." When mother tells them they would become different as they aged, that they would develop "teats and beards", they become anxious. They plan to arrest the passage of time in order to avoid any differences appearing between them. They do this using ritual practices (as did the twins in *Gemini*)—a bodily enactment that echoes their visceral entanglement with each other.

These literary twins elucidate another common element in twins in literature—their visceral attachment to each other, accompanied by the terror of separateness and differentiation, which are felt to be life threatening. The need to balance individuality and twin-relatedness emerges clearly, while focusing on the difficulties or impossibility of doing so in twins who are so deeply enmeshed through their need to survive a very hostile world. For them the twinship is their only liferaft.

Arundhati Roy also writes about opposite sex twins in *The God of Small Things* (1997). This is a complex novel about the caste system in India, as followed through the lives of twins Estha and Rahel. The central idea in this twinship is the intimate understanding between the twins, the feeling that neither twin has ever found the level of understanding with others that they have between them. Thus here too we get a sense of the deep unconscious bond that exists between twins, and the effects this has on a sense of identity.

Estha and Rahel operate as a self-sufficient twin unit. They are forced to separate when Rahel is sent away. Estha experiences the agony of the loss of her twin brother viscerally as she doubles up in pain and screams at his departure. In his new family, Rahel becomes mute, "psychically empty of himself". He takes on the role of his sister, a female role, where he cooks and cleans. Thus he feels he has not lost his twin, but has become her.

They meet again as adults, forlornly, and they lie side by side like two spoons. Inevitably incest follows as they find each other again, and merge in their renewed twinship. Their sibling incest acts as a refuge from a too traumatic world. Each longs to replace the self with this intimacy, after the trauma of their brutal separation. They create a "pre-egoic comfort of other as self", in a two-as-one boundary-less state.

So, these literary opposite sex twins have a visceral bond, like *The Fahrenheit Twins*; but unlike them, they have differentiated sexually and the theme of incest is played out as an indication of the depth of their intimacy and the deep need they have for each other. In other books (*The Black Hill, Gemini, The Solid Mandala*) the male twins also have an incestuous relationship as one aspect of their intense closeness. Two become one, as if in doing so the struggle to survive or differentiate is wiped out by merging bliss.

Twins as split selves

Philip Pullman's understanding of the nature of the splitting of the self has extended from his acclaimed trilogy, *His Dark Materials*, to his latest book, *The Good Man Jesus and the Scoundrel Christ* (2010) in which he applies this theme to a story about actual twins. He explores the nature of identity within the context of powerful inner and outer forces in society. In this book, we encounter the themes of the duality of man, of heaven and earth again, of divine and mortal, replaying the Castor and Pollux (known together as the Dioscuri) story in a new format. There are other stories about Jesus Christ being a twin, ancient stories, one claiming that St Thomas was the twin of Jesus Christ, where *Toma* means twin in Aramaic.

In this book, the character of Jesus is divided into opposing personas as Pullman imaginatively portrays the dilemma that so arouses him (Pullman): the disparity between the recorded teachings of Jesus, and the way they have been appropriated and misused by his so-called followers.

Pullman, who says clearly that it is *a story*, writes that Jesus had a twin brother called Christ. Jesus was the strong healthy baby, quiet and calm, at ease with himself, while Christ was a small, weak, and sickly child whom his mother protected and favoured. When the twins were born, Mary fed Christ first because he was weaker, and it was while she was still feeding the more robust Jesus, as Christ lay in the feeding trough, that the shepherds approached. Then the astrologers bearing gifts to the promised "Messiah" (Christ means Messiah), arrived from the East having been told to look for the child sent by God, who would be lying in a feeding trough.

As they grow up, each twin follows a different path. Jesus is more down to earth. He learns carpentry from his father and is at ease with the others. He passionately embraces reality, and maintains a capacity to think rather than just obey the doctrines. He has a radical vision that frightens the authorities. He has the wisdom and understanding to help others who are distressed without resorting to magical cures. He has the strength, in the Garden of Gethsemane, to realise he has to bear the burden on his own and, according to Pullman, abandons his faith, believing God has deserted him.

Christ is the weaker, self-righteous, fearful twin who shadows Jesus, trying to persuade him to accept miracles and magical solutions, which Jesus refutes. Christ is very taken in by religious texts and believes in "the mirage of a world forever safe from doubt and permeated by the benign if somewhat capricious presence of a God who reinforces his commands with—well, magic" (Williams, 2010). Christ is an uncertain figure who is heavily influenced by a Stranger (a figure who stands for the corruptor of the ordinary truthfulness of Jesus by importing external facts). The Stranger tells Christ to record and edit everything that Jesus says and does. The religious authorities need Christ to do this in order to embody their truth rather than that of Jesus, and they believe that Jesus and Christ combined together would be a miracle. The Stranger, who holds so much influence over Christ, tells him that he is the missing part of himself, a part called Jesus.

The Stranger eventually prompts Christ to betray his brother Jesus. Christ does this initially as when he disguises himself as Satan in the wilderness, and he urges Jesus to provide miracles to help persuade his followers to believe in the imminence of the coming "Kingdom of God". Later, and finally, he betrays Jesus as the Judas figure who fatally kisses his twin brother to identify him to the soldiers.

Jesus dies on the cross after being betrayed by Christ/Judas. His resurrection is not a miracle, but a stunt organised by the Stranger. Christ achieves this by removing Jesus's body from the tomb, and then Christ lies in the tomb and takes the place of the dead Jesus, who then appears to have risen from death. Christ impersonates Jesus to Mary Magdalene, who has arrived to mourn Jesus. He is aided in doing this because he has always been so nondescript a figure that no one recognises him or takes any notice of him.

Pullman's primary aim in using twins in this book is to describe his views about religion, authority, and the individual, within a society that places enormous pressures on individuals to conform in particular ways, and that twists or embroiders truths to suit its messages—propaganda. It is a masterful and deeply thoughtful comment on religion per se, and the way religion is used to control its followers. He does not play on the common themes of inter-changeability and sameness, until the death of Jesus, when Christ is able to impersonate Jesus because they look so alike, and because Christ has always been a nonentity, unseen as a person of little merit.

Different though these twins are, they are tied together as a pair. They are like two sides of a coin, strong and weak, good and evil. But these twins are not portrayed as in the older writings about the double as an expression of the division of body and soul. The split is more a mortal affair. Christ is a pathetic weak side, easily led astray by powerful forces, perhaps representing the side that Jesus struggles with in the Garden of Gethsemane—the wish to give in to dependency at the expense of morality and truthfulness. In contrast, Jesus is strong and maintains his integrity though not without deep personal struggles.

Female twins as mystery

Her Fearful Symmetry by Audrey Niffenegger (2009) is a typical book about twins in that we encounter a very stereotyped view of twins with their lack of individual identity, their soul sharing, their inter-changeability in appearance, and the usual division of weak and strong assets. There are two sets of twins in the story, the blonde, looka-like twin girls who come to London, and their mother and her twin sister. Audrey Niffenegger highlights the difficulty for one twin to allow the other to be separate, except through death, at which time the other continues to exist as a present ghost. There is great play on confusion and repetition between the mother and her twin sister, who become mixed up and agree to change identities—after one twin's boyfriend has made the other twin pregnant—with the twin girls. When she dies, the other twin leaves her inheritance to her twin nieces/daughters. There is a ghost of the dead aunt enticing one of the twin girls away from life, and interchanges between the dead twin aunt and twin daughters. It is all set against a background of Highgate Cemetery with lots of saving and swapping of souls.

I have mentioned this book here because it is typical of much of the literature about twins, using twins as a vehicle for more supernatural themes that play on ghosts and spirits, and in some ways echo the earlier romantic works about twins.

In *A Spanish Lover* by Joanna Trollope (1993), we again have twin women who consider themselves to be individually "half a twin" (p. 11). They seem to be locked in a seesaw where one twin succeeds as the other fails. Lizzie and Frances are twins and Lizzie feels chained to Frances's innermost self. There is a second set of twins in Lizzie's son Alistair, whose twin died at birth. Lizzie and Frances know each other's thoughts and together make up a joint wholeness, a rich round person, two pieces of a jigsaw—they have to fit together, so are complementary rather than the same shape.

In Lizzie's view, she and Frances had all the conspiratorial closeness of twins, and together formed part of a unit, a joint wholeness. But as Frances began to separate out of the twinship and become her own person, she no longer feels bound to Lizzie by some primordial cord, leading to a decline in Lizzie. They do separate in the end as each estab-lishes a sense of individuality, and they reconcile happily as reunited twins who both have their individual lives.

This is essentially a love story about an independent woman, and the theme of twins is a device to hold the sense of a lack of development as an individual in each of the women, using the usual views that twins have to share success or failure, and divide their personal capacities.

Many twin books are written to beguile the reader into the mystery and tensions of doubles in the flesh. *The Thirteenth Tale* by Diane Setterfield (2006) is just such a book. It is a good and gripping read with all the ingredients to keep us turning the pages, and it uses the commonplace ideas about twins, their being outside the normal range of development, being encapsulated in a private world no one else can enter, with a magical and unbreakable bond.

In this book, twins are regarded as half-persons and there is a belief that singletons must appear to twins as half-persons, as amputees. There are two sets of twins: Margaret Lea, the biographer, discovers she had a conjoined twin who died at birth after they were separated—the twin was parasitic and could not survive alone. This accounts for her persistent deep sense of longing and a feeling that something profound is missing, of her seeing or feeling a pale shadow, seeing herself reflected in the window, or a ghostly presence passing by. She is weighed down with a sense of loss, sorrow, and loneliness.

As a lone twin, Margaret believes she is half dead, "exiled in the world of the living by day, while at night my soul cleaves to its twin in a shadowy limbo" (p. 181). Margaret's mother was unable either to mourn for her dead baby twin or to pay attention to the living one. As a result, mother lived her life as an emotional invalid, unable to celebrate the birth of her live child because the other twin died. Margaret wonders why her life meant less to her mother than her sister's death. (The difficulties for parents in mourning a dead twin and celebrating the other live twin are clearly expressed in this novel.) With this lack of attention from mother, Margaret believes that bereaved twins are half souls. She creates a substitute double by removing curtains so she can see her reflection in the window.

At the end of the book, she is momentarily reunited with her dead twin and she then feels at peace. Her dead twin, Moira, comes to her.

> Her cheek against mine, her arm across my shoulders, my hand at her waist. Scar to scar we touched, and all my questions faded as I felt her blood flow with mine, her heart beat with mine. It was a moment of wonderment, great and calm; and I knew that

I *remembered* this feeling. It has been locked inside me, closed
away, and now she had come and released it. This blissful circuitry.
This oneness that had once been ordinary, and was today, now that
I had recovered it, miraculous. (Setterfield, 2006, p. 453)

Her dead twin had come to say goodbye, so what we see is a process that
moves from merging to mourning when the survivor has been reunited
with and then relinquishes her dead twin. Now her life is her own.

The other twins in the book are Adeline and Emmeline March, twin
girls who grow up in a household of absent or disinterested parents, with
a housekeeper and gardener who can not cope with them. They rule the
roost and are deviant and unsocialisable. Adeline and Emmeline are
enmeshed twins who share a secret language and they divide attributes
between them. Adeline March is a difficult, wild twin, an angry and
violent girl, "the girl in the mist". Emmeline is regarded as the calm,
complacent twin, who is generally presumed by most to be mentally
retarded because she is dominated by Adeline and passively complies
with her. However, it gradually emerges that Emmeline is an intelligent
and compassionate person who might have led a normal life, even perhaps married someday.

In the absence of parental attachment, Adeline and Emmeline depend
on each other for their development, thus being wholly shaped by their
twin relationship. When the local doctor and a new governess together
decide that the twin girls need to be separated in order to develop nor-
mally, the result is catastrophic. The severance of the twin bond leads to
a total collapse, emotionally, in both the girls, similar to the description
of children severed from their daemons in Philip Pullman's trilogy.
Adeline describes how without her sister she was nothing, no one, just
the shell of a person. The girls became limp, unresponsive, and emotionally dead, until they are reunited.

One twist in the story reveals that there is a third girl, found living
in the grounds of the estate, a shadowy abandoned half-sister who also
looks so like the twins that at times she plays the part of one of them.
It transpires that, contrary to the assumption for much of the book that
author Vida Winter, about whom Margaret Lea is writing a biography, is the twin Adeline, the author Vida Winter is actually this third
half-sister.

The secrets unravel and what the biographer finds is that Emmeline
became pregnant and Adeline was murderously jealous of the baby and

planned to kill him in a fire. Half-sister Vida Winter, however, watches her and rescues the baby. Vida Winter and the person she thinks is Emmeline get into a fight as the fire burns and Emmeline goes in to rescue the baby. But Vida Winter has already replaced the baby with a blanket roll and she tries to rescue Emmeline, grabbing her and pulling her out of the fire that demolishes the house. Later the bones of the other twin are discovered in the ruins of the house. There is a confusion of identities in the disastrous fire that destroys the home of the twins, and kills one of the twins. But doubts arise—whom has Vida Winter rescued? Emmeline or Adeline? Who is the badly burned and very disturbed twin who is found to be living in the other wing of Vida Winter's house, and who is sometimes heard moaning and singing late at night?

With Adeline and Emmeline, we have twins who are deeply enmeshed, one dominating the other and utterly intolerant of any interference in the twinship. They are bound together in a deathly embrace, neither believing they can exist without the other. They are bound in duty and intense rivalry. Any hope of a productive life is stifled, but by subterfuge, the baby, a product of the glimmer of separateness, is saved. It takes the third half-sister to inject some humanity and individuality into the closed system of the twinship. The half-sister represents the objectivity of someone outside the enmeshed twinship but connected with it.

In contrast, the biographer Margaret Lea is able eventually to mourn her lost twin as she has had a loving father who has provided a framework for her development despite the absence of an engaged, loving mother, and the absence of her twin.

Diane Setterfield has skilfully portrayed the difficulties for parents of twins when one dies, and the different aspects of twin relationships and the possibilities for growth and development in each twin, where the twins can tolerate separateness and the process of becoming individuals. The internalised loving father would be an important structure helping the biographer develop and grieve for her lost twin even though mother is so unavailable and so focused on the dead twin. The imprisoned, burned twin in the other cut-off wing represents the stifling grip of an enmeshed twinship and the searing wound experienced when separated. The rage and pain can only be split off and distanced because the surviving twin has no capacity for mourning and thence re-integrating her lost self.

In conclusion, we find that twins in literature represent many of our current and past dilemmas about identity, sameness, difference, and relatedness. In the more simplistic writings, they may represent stereotypes, but in those books that delve deeper, twins can express a much more complex understanding of our nature. They may represent different levels of our psychic functioning, like unconscious hidden desires versus our conscious socialised selves. They may also represent split-off aspects of the self, either because we disown something we don't like, or to preserve it from other danger. In some of the books I have written about here, the depth and potency of the twin relationship has been clearly described, elucidating the dynamics of the twin relationship and our perceptions of twins.

In some books, the twins remain stuck in their enmeshed twin relationship; in others there is a greater degree of resolution of personal identity for each of the twins. Themes of narcissism and incest are common in the literature on twins, and the search for identity both individually and as a twin is a potent theme throughout. Separateness and commonality are persistent dialectical dilemmas and are felt to be essential to the social nature of man. Twins incarnate these dilemmas and are thus a very useful tool in literature.

Twins in literature are also used to explore issues about the possibilities life offers us and what we, individually, do with life events. Using the device of twins who begin life together within a particular environment, we see for each of the literary twins (whether MZ, DZ, or different sex) how their lives diverge and differ, what choices each twin makes, and how this affects their development as a person. As Ann Morgan (2016) suggests, twins in literature "throw up questions about our uniqueness, and the chances and choices that make us who we are". Twins show us how we might have taken different paths in life and may have been different. The issue of doubles or near-sameness is used to explore identity in terms of what we might have become. Two similar people (twins) born at the same time and perhaps sharing a high degree of genetic identity, take different paths. So given who we are, might we have made different choices that would have led us somewhere different?

CONCLUDING COMMENTS

There is a great deal of information and material in this book and it might be helpful to draw together the main issues I have written about.

The focus of the book is on the internal dynamics of twin relationships, their origins and the factors that influence them, and our enduring fascination with twins based on our own early experiences.

Twins have a lifelong internal relationship that may shift from the narcissistic end of the spectrum—where they feel enmeshed with each other in the twinship, and dependent on it—to the companionable area where they continue to regard the twinship as important but are able to find individual identities and separate lives.

The deep internal relationship between twins is based on early sensate experiences, not only the early experiences with mother, but importantly the biological resonances and sensory experiences twins have with each other, beginning in utero. The inter-twin dynamics may be affected and sometimes reinforced by external factors, starting with parental input, siblings, and the wider outside world. Our perceptions of twins will affect the development of the twins within the twinship.

Several themes outlining the factors that affect the development of twins have permeated the book:

1. Between the twins:
   a. early sensate experiences between them
   b. companionship—an unparalleled closeness
   c. rivalry—intense competition
   d. complex early and later patterns of relating that are different from other siblings
   e. identity development as both twins and separate individuals, and the establishment of discrete boundaries between them.
2. Between the twins and mother, father, siblings, and others:
   a. attention given to each
   b. language development according to maternal speech patterns
   c. individuality dependent on quality of personal attention to each
   d. separateness and togetherness—a balance in the twinship in relation to their other attachments.
3. The projections by all those outside the twin relationship based on our own early experiences and projections of these onto the twin pair.

Examples of the nature and the perception of twin relationships and development are traced in society, in literature, and around the world.

REFERENCES

Aitkenhead, D. (2011). Eagle sisters fly high at Westminster. *Guardian*, 12 April.

Auster, P. (1987). *New York Trilogy*. London: Faber.

Beebe, B., Lachmann, F. M., & Jaffe, J. (1997). Mother–Infant Interaction Structures and Presymbolic Self- and Object Representations. *Psychoanalytic Dialogues, 7*: 133–182.

Bick, E. (1968). The experience of the skin in early object-relations. *International Journal of Psycho-Analysis, 49*: 484–486.

Boklage, C. E. (1995). The frequency and survivability of natural twin conceptions. In: A. Hayton (Ed.), *Untwinned. Perspectives on the Death of a Twin before Birth* (pp. 94–98). Waltham Cross: Wren.

Bryan, E. M. (1992). Language development in twins. In: *Twins and Higher Multiples: A guide to their Nature and Nurture*. Sevenoaks: Edward Arnold.

Bryan, E. M. (1999). The death of a twin. In: A. Sandbank (Ed.), *Twin and Triplet Psychology. A Professional Guide to Working with Multiples* (pp. 186–199). London: Routledge.

Burlingham, D. T. (1963). A study of identical twins—their analytic material compared with existing observation data of their early childhood. *Psychoanalytic Study of the Child, 18*: 367–423.

Butler, S., McMahon, C., & Ungerer, J. (2002). *Infant and Child Development, 12:* 129–143 (2003). http://onlinelibrary.wiley.com/doi/10.1002/icd.272/abstract [last accessed 19 April 2016].

Case, B. J. (1993). *Living Without Your Twin.* Portland, OR: Tibbutt.

Chamberlain, D. B. (2013). The fetal senses, a classic view. *Birth Psychology,* Association for Prenatal and Perinatal Psychology and Health. http://birthpsychology.com/free-article/fetal-senses-classical-view [last accessed 19 April 2016].

Chatwin, B. (1982). *On the Black Hill.* London: Jonathan Cape.

Coles, P. (2014, May). Siblings really matter. Paper presented at the meeting of the Institute of Child Mental Health.

Collins English Dictionary (6th edn) (2003). Glasgow: HarperCollins.

de Nooy, J. (2005). Twins in Contemporary Literature and Culture. Look Twice. London: Palgrave.

Diskin, S. (2001). *The End of the Twins. A Memoir of Losing a Brother.* New York: Overlook.

Dostoevsky, F. (1846). *The Double.* London: Hesperus, 2004.

Down, C. M. (2006). The surviving twin: psychological, emotional and spiritual impacts of having experienced a death before birth. In: A. Hayton (Ed.), *Untwinned. Perspectives on the Death of a Twin before Birth* (pp. 64–74). Waltham Cross: Wren.

Dundy, E. (1985). *Elvis and Gladys. The Genesis of the King.* London: Weidenfeld & Nicolson.

Faber, M. (2005). *The Fahrenheit Twins.* Edinburgh: Canongate.

Farmer, P. (1996). *Two, or: the Book of Twins and Doubles.* London: Virago.

Farroni, T., Csibra, G., Simion, F., & Johnson, M. (2002). Eye contact detection in humans from birth. *Proceedings of the National Academy of Sciences of the United States of America, 99*(14): 9605.

Farroni, T., Johnson, M., & Csibra, G. (2004). Mechanisms of eye gaze perception during infancy. *Journal of Cognitive Neuroscience, 16*(8): 1320–1326.

Freud, S. (1912–1913). *Totem and Taboo. S. E., 13:* 1. London: Hogarth.

Freud, S. (1916–1917). Introductory Lectures on Psycho-Analysis. *S. E., 15–16.* London: Hogarth.

Freud, S. (1917e). Mourning and Melancholia. *S. E., 14:* 239. London: Hogarth.

Freud, S. (1919h). The "Uncanny". *S. E., 17:* 219. London: Hogarth.

Glenn, J. (1986). Twinship themes and fantasies in the work of Thornton Wilder. *Psychoanalytic Study of the Child, 41:* 627–651.

Graves, R., & Patai, R. (1992). *Hebrew Myths.* Detroit, MI: Wayne State University Press.

Grossman, S. (2013). http://time.com/author/samantha-grossman/ [last accessed 19 April 2016].

Guardian (2007). Shaffer twins had identity crisis over name. 30 January. http://hitchwiki.com/h/3551 [last accessed 19 April 2016].

Hall, J. G. (2003). Twinning. *The Lancet, 362*: 735–743.

Harris, J. R. (1906). *The Cult of the Heavenly Twins*. Cambridge: Cambridge University Press.

Hastings, J. (1921). *Encyclopaedia of Religion and Ethics*. Volume 21, pp. 491–500. Edinburgh: T & T Clark.

Hogg, J. (1824). *The Private Memoirs and Confessions of a Justified Sinner*. Oxford: Oxford University Press, 1999.

Hough, A., & Thompson, P. (2013). Woman with multiple wombs "pregnant" with two babies that are not twins. Telegraph, 30 October.

Jeffreys, M. D. W. (1963). The cult of twins among some African tribes. *South African Journal of Science, 59*(4): 97–107.

Joseph, J. (2004). *The Gene Illusion—Genetic Research in Psychiatry and Psychology Under the Microscope*. New York: Algora.

Klein, M. (1963). On the sense of loneliness. In: *Envy and Gratitude and Other Works* (pp. 300–313). London: Hogarth, 1980.

Knatchbull, T. (2010). *From a Clear Blue Sky*. London: Hutchinson.

Kristof, A. (1997). *The Notebook, The Proof, The Third Lie*. New York: Grove.

Larousse Encyclopedia of Mythology (1959). London: Paul Hamlyn.

Lash, J. (1993). *Twins and the Double*. London: Thames & Hudson.

Levi-Strauss, C. (1955). The structural study of myth. *Journal of American Folklore, 68*: 113–144.

Lewin, V. (2004). *The Twin in the Transference*. London: Karnac, 2014 (2nd edn).

Macdonald, H. (2014). *H is for Hawk*. London: Jonathan Cape.

Milton, J. (1644). Areopagitica. In: *Areopagitica and Other Prose Works*. London: Dent.

Mitchell, J. (2000). *Madmen and Medusas. Reclaiming Hysteria*. New York: Basic.

Mitchell, J. (2003). *Siblings*. Cambridge: Polity.

Morgan, A. (2016). The power of two. *Guardian*, 26 January.

Niffenegger, A. (2009). *Her Fearful Symmetry*. London: Jonathan Cape.

Nightingale, B. (2004). Quoted in *Encyclopedia of World Biography*. www.encyclopedia.com/topic/Peter_Shaffer.aspx [last accessed 19 April 2016].

Nyqvist, K. H. (1998). Co-bedding twins: a developmentally supportive care strategy. *Journal of Obstetric, Gynecologic and Neonatal Nursing, 27*(4): 450–456.

Ogden, T. (2005). *This Art of Psychoanalysis. Dreaming Undreamt Dreams and Interrupted Cries*. London: Routledge.

Pearson, J. (1972). *The Profession of Violence. The Rise and Fall of the Kray Twins*. London: HarperCollins, 1995.

Pearson, J. (1977). The Lords of the Underworld. Independent, 14 June 1997.

Pector, E. (2002). Twin death and mourning worldwide: a review of the literature. *Twin Research, 5*(3): 196–205.

Pector, E. (2006). Twin traditions worldwide for life, death and mourning. In: A. Hayton (Ed.), *Untwinned. Perspectives on the Death of a Twin before Birth* (pp. 15–27). Waltham Cross: Wren.

Piontelli, A. (2002). *Twins: From Foetus to Child*. London: Routledge.

Plato (360 BCE). Symposium. In: *The Essential Plato*. B. Jowett (Trans.) (1871). New York: Book-of-the-Month Club, 1999.

Poe, E. A. (1839a). *The Fall of the House of Usher*. New York: Viking, 1960.

Poe, E. A. (1839b). *William Wilson*. New York: Viking, 1960.

Proner, K. (2000). Protomental synchrony: some thoughts on the earliest identification processes in a neonate. *The International Journal of Infant Observation, 3*: 55–63.

Pullman, P. (1995). *His Dark Materials*. London: Scholastic.

Pullman, P. (2009). Questions and Answers, 6 March. http://www.philip-pullman.com/qas?searchtext=&page=5 [last accessed 19 April 2016].

Pullman, P. (2010). *The Good Man Jesus and the Scoundrel Christ*. Edinburgh: Canongate.

Raphael-Leff, J. (1990). If Oedipus was an Egyptian. *International Review of Psycho-Analysis, 17*: 309–335.

Roy, A. (1997). *The God of Small Things*. London: Flamingo.

Royle, N. (2014). Twins and Doubles. BBC World Service, 6 January.

Rustin, M., & Rustin, M. (2004). The siblings of Measure for Measure and Twelfth Night. In: P. Coles (Ed.), *Sibling Relationships* (pp. 118–119). London: Karnac, 2006.

Sand, G. (2012). *Fanchon the Cricket*. Memphis, TE: General. [Originally *La Petite Fadette*, 1849.]

Schore, A. N. (1994). *Affect Regulation and the Origin of the Self: the Neurobiology of Emotional Development*. Hillsdale, NJ: Erlbaum.

Setterfield, D. (2006). *The Thirteenth Tale*. London: Orion.

Shakespeare, W. (1594). *The Comedy of Errors*. London: Oxford University Press, 1952.

Shakespeare, W. (1596). *King John*. London: Oxford University Press, 1952.

Shakespeare, W. (1601). *Twelfth Night*. London: Oxford University Press, 1952.

Sipes, N. J., & Sipes, J. S. (1998). *Dancing Naked in Front of the Fridge. And Other Lessons from Twins*. Beverly, MA: Fair Winds.

Spector, T. (2012). *Identically Different: Why You Can Change Your Genes*. London: Weidenfeld.

Stevenson, R. L. (1886). *The Strange Case of Dr. Jekyll and Mr. Hyde*. London: Penguin, 2002.

Swanson, P. B. (2001, July). When is a twin not a twin? Paper presented at the meeting of the 10th International Congress on Twin Studies, London.

Telegraph (2016). George Cooper (obituary). 16 April.

Thorpe, K., Greenwood R., Eivers A., & Rutter, M. (2001). Prevalence and developmental course of "secret language". *International Journal of Language and Communication Disorders, 36*(1): 43–62.

Tournier, M. (1975). *Gemini*. Baltimore, MD: Johns Hopkins, 1998.

Trollope, J. (1993). *A Spanish Lover*. London: Bloomsbury.

Turner, L. (2012). Robin Gibb "reunited with twin": Brother Barry's emotional tribute at Bee Gee's funeral. Independent, 8 June.

Twain, M. (1881). *The Prince and the Pauper*. Marston Gate: Providence, 2013.

Twain M. (1894). *Pudd'nhead Wilson and those extraordinary twins*. New York: Norton, 2005.

Vivona, J. M. (2010). Siblings, transference, and the lateral dimension of psychic life. *Psychoanalytic Psychology, 27*: 8–26.

Wallace, M. (1996). *The Silent Twins*. London: Vintage.

White, P. (1966). *The Solid Mandala*. London: Penguin, 1969.

White, P. (1981). *Flaws in the Glass*. London: Jonathan Cape.

Wilde, O. (1890). *The Picture of Dorian Gray*. Kindle edn: G Books, 4 December 2011.

Wilder, T. (1973). Theophilus North. New York: Harper & Row.

Wilder, T. (2015). Thornton Wilder society website: www.twildersociety. org/works/theophilus-north/ [last accessed 19 April 2016].

Wilder, T. B. (1927). *The Bridge of San Luis Rey*. London: Penguin, 2000.

Williams, C. (2014). *Black Valley*. London: Macmillan.

Williams, R. (2010). Review of *The Good Man Jesus and the Scoundrel Christ* by Philip Pullman. *Guardian*, 3 April.

Winnicott, D. W. (1953). Transitional objects and transitional phenomena— a study of the first not-me possession. *International Journal of Psycho-Analysis, 34*: 89–97.

Winnicott, D. W. (1956). Primary maternal preoccupation. *Through Paediatrics to Psycho-Analysis. The International Psycho-Analytical Library, 100*: 300–305. London: Hogarth, 1975.

Woodward, J. (1998). *The Lone Twin. A Study in Bereavement and Loss*. London: Free Association.

Wright, L. (1997). *Twins. Genes, Environment and the Mystery of Identity*. London: Weidenfeld.

FURTHER READING

Ball, H. L., & Hill, C. M. (1996). Twin infanticide. *Current Anthropology, 37*(5): 856–863.

Bascom, W. R. (1951). The Yoruba in Cuba. *Nigeria, 37*: 14–20.

Bion, W. R. (1962). *Learning from Experience*. London: Tavistock.

Blessing, D. (2014). Casting a long shadow: implications of sibling loss. In: K. Skrzypek, B. Maciejewska, & Z. Stadnicka-Dmitriew (Eds.), *Siblings: Envy and Rivalry, Co-existence and Concern* (p. 137). London: Karnac.

Bryan, E. M. (1995). The death of a twin. In: A. Hayton (Ed.), *Untwinned. Perspectives on the Death of a Twin before Birth*. Waltham Cross: Wren.

Carter, H. (2005). Three sisters unite for surrogate birth. *Guardian*, 25 October, p. 5.

Corney, G. (1975). Mythology and customs associated with twins. In: I. MacGillivray, P. P. S. Nylander, & G. Corney (Eds.), *Human Multiple Reproduction*. London: Saunders.

Courlander, H. (1973). How the twins came among the Yorubas. In: *Tales of Yoruba Gods and Heroes* (pp. 137–141). New York: Crown.

Dalton Hall (2000–2003). Ere Ibejis: Yoruba twin figures from the Bryn Mawr College Collection. www.brynmawr.edu/collections/Exhibitions/exh-ibeji.shtml [last accessed 19 April 2016].

Davison, S. (1992). Mother, other and self—love and rivalry for twins in their first year of life. *International Review of Psycho-Analysis, 19*: 359–374.

Devereaux, G. (1941). Mohave beliefs concerning twins. *American Anthropologist NS, 43*: 573–592.

Evans-Pritchard, E. E. (1936). Customs and beliefs relating to twins among the Nilotic Nuer. *Uganda Journal, 3*: 230–238.

Evans-Pritchard, E. E. (1956). The problem of symbols. In: *Nuer Religion*. Oxford: Clarendon.

Farroni, T., Johnson, M., Menon, E., Zulian, L., Faraguna, D., & Csibra, G. (2005). Newborns' preference for face-relevant stimuli: effects of contrast polarity. *Proceedings of the National Academy of Sciences of the United States of America, 102*(47): 17245–17250.

Ganger, J. (2005). Are twins delayed in language development? http://www.mit.edu/~mittwins/delaylit.html [last accessed 19 April, 2016].

Halcrow, S., Tayles, N., Inglis, R., & Higham, C. (2012). Newborn twins from prehistoric mainland Southeast Asia: birth, death and personhood. *Antiquity, 86*: 838–852.

Hankoff, L. D. (1977). Why the healing gods are twins. *Yale Journal of Biology and Medicine, 50*: 307–319.

Harvey, K. (2003). What vanishing twins may be telling us. In: A. Hayton (Ed.), *Untwinned. Perspectives on the Death of a Twin before Birth*. Waltham Cross: Wren.

Hayton, A. (2007). *Untwinned. Perspectives on the death of a twin before birth*. Waltham Cross: Wren.

Joseph, J. (2008). Separated twins and the genetics of personality differences: a critique. *American Journal of Psychology, 114*(1): 1–30. http://www.jstor.org/stable/1423378 [last accessed 19 April 2016].

Knight, W. N. (2004). *Autobiography in Shakespeare's Plays. Twins at the Inns of Court*. Oxford: Peter Lang.

Lacan, J. (1949). The mirror stage as formative of the function of the I as revealed in psychoanalytic experience. In: *Ecrits. A Selection* (pp. 1–7). London: Tavistock, 1977.

Leroy, F., Olaleye-Oruene, T., Koeppen-Schomerus, G., & Bryan, E. (2002). Yoruba customs and beliefs pertaining to twins. *Twin Research, 5*(2): 132–136.

Loeb, E. (1956). The twin cult in the old and new world. Miscellanea Paul Rivet Octogenario Dictata, 1958, XXXI Congreso Internacional de Americanistas, Universidad Nacional Autonoma de Mexico.

Mogford-Bevan, K. (1999). Twins and their language development. In: A. Sandbank (Ed.), *Twin and Triplet Psychology. A professional Guide to Working with Multiples* (pp. 36–60). London: Routledge.

O'Hagan, S. (2002). Hungry for fame. (When twins adopt one identity in the name of art, that's challenging enough. But when they weigh the same together as one healthy person, that's really shocking.) Observer, 17 February.

Omari-Tunkara, M. S. (2005). *Manipulating the Sacred: Yoruba Art, Ritual, and Resistance in Brazilian Candoble*. Detroit, MI: Wayne State University Press.

Oruene, T. O. (1985). The cult of the ibeji as reflected in the oriki ibeji. *Anthropos, 80*: 230–237.

Pharoah, P. O. D., & Adi, Y. (2000). Consequences of in-utero death in a twin pregnancy. *Lancet, 355*: 1597–1602.

Piontelli, A. (1999). Twins in utero: temperament development and intertwine behaviour before and after birth. In: A. Sandbank (Ed.), *Twin and Triplet Psychology. A Professional Guide to Working with Multiples* (pp. 7–18). London: Routledge.

Quinodoz, J.-M. (1993). *The Taming of Solitude. Separation Anxiety in Psychoanalysis*. London: Routledge.

Rank, O. (1971). *The Double*. Chapel Hill, NC: University of North Carolina Press.

Sandbank, A. (Ed.) (1999). Personality, identity and family relationships. In: *Twin and Triplet Psychology. A Professional Guide to Working with Multiples*. London: Routledge.

Saramago, J. (2002). *The Double*. Boston, MA: Houghton Mifflin Harcourt, 2004.

Schapera, I. (1962). *The Bantu-Speaking Tribes of South Africa. An Ethnographical Survey*. Cape Town: Mashew Miller.

Siemon, M. (1980). The separation-individuation process in adult twins. *American Journal of Psychotherapy, 34*(3): 387–400.

Stewart, E. A. (2000). *Exploring Twins. Towards a Social Analysis of Twinship*. London: Macmillan.

Ulrich, G. (1996). Thunderchildren: Yoruba twin figure carvings from Nigeria. In: *Lore*. Milwaukee, WI: Milwaukee Public Museum.

Van der Wee, A. (Dir.) (2012). *Lone Twin*. Montreal: Wild Heart Productions and Storyline Entertainment.

Veith, I. (1960). Twin birth: blessing or disaster. A Japanese view. *International Journal of Social Psychiatry, 6*: 230–236.

Watzlawik, M., Kriebel, S., Wiedeau, S., & Deutsch, W. (2004). Dyadic identity development. An analysis of observational data and parental ratings. *Twin Research*, 11 June.

Winestine, M. C. (1968). Twinship and psychological differentiation. *Journal of Child Psychiatry, 8*: 436–455.

Winnicott, D. W. (1971). Mirror-role of mother and family in child development. In: *Playing and Reality* (p. 149). Abingdon: Routledge, 2005.

INDEX